The Complete Electronic Percussion Book

by David Crombie.
Additional material by Mark Jenkins and Bob Henrit.

Amsco Publications.
London/New York/Sydney

Exclusive Distributors:

Music Sales Limited
8/9 Frith Street, London, W1V 5TZ, England.

Music Sales Pty. Limited
27 Clarendon Street, Artarmon, Sydney, NSW 2064, Australia.

Music Sales Corporation
24 East 22nd Street, New York 10010, N.Y. USA.

This book © Copyright 1987 by Amsco Publications.
UK ISBN 0.7119.1126.6
US ISBN 0.8256.1092.3
Order No. AM 65772

Art directed by Mike Bell.
Book designed by Sands Straker Limited.
Cover designed by Pearce Marchbank.
Illustration by Mark Straker.

The author wishes to acknowledge the assistance of:
Mark Jenkins.
Bob Henrit.
Dave Simmons, Geoff Howorth, Andy Skirrow at Simmons Electronics Limited.
Yamaha Kemble Limited for supplying photographs and rhythm patterns.
Roland (UK) Limited for photographs and rhythm patterns.
Rob Castle at KORG (UK) Limited.
Martin Brady at Casio Computer Co. Limited.

Music Sales complete catalogue lists thousands of titles and is free from
your local music book shop, or direct from Music Sales Limited.
Please send 50p in stamps for postage to
Music Sales Limited, 8/9 Frith Street, London W1V 5TZ.

Printed in England by
The Anchor Press Limited, Tiptree, Essex.

The Complete Electronic Percussion Book.

This book is the first to deal comprehensively with the technological revolution that has transformed the percussion world over the past ten years.

The various chapters are aimed at:

1) the acoustic drummer wanting a clear and precise guide to these new devices;

2) the non-drummer needing information on how to program these instruments in order to create an effective rhythm track;

and designed to cover two distinct categories of percussive instrumentation:

1) The electronic drum kit.

2) The drum machine/rhythm unit/ percussion computer.

The common theme of all the percussive instruments dealt with in this book is that all the sounds are electronically generated, i.e. an electrical signal is generated by the instrument, and an amplifier and loudspeaker arrangement of some kind is required in order to hear the resulting sound.

It is, therefore, an advantage to have some knowledge of the fundamentals of sound and also a small insight into the world of electronics, if for no other reason than to know what your local music store owner is talking about when he asks "Will you be needing a ROM or RAM pack with your instrument (sir)?".

The drum is undoubtedly the earliest form of musical instrument, yet it has only been over the past decade or so that there has been any significant development in the world of percussive hardware. We may have utilised strangely shaped, ergonomically more suited, varieties of tambourine; we may have tried the new style "screw-on" head drum kits; we may even have played bizarrely shaped drum kits more like fog horns than conventional drums, but only with the marriage of electronics and percussion will we have witnessed a totally new form of instrumentation.

INTRODUCTION

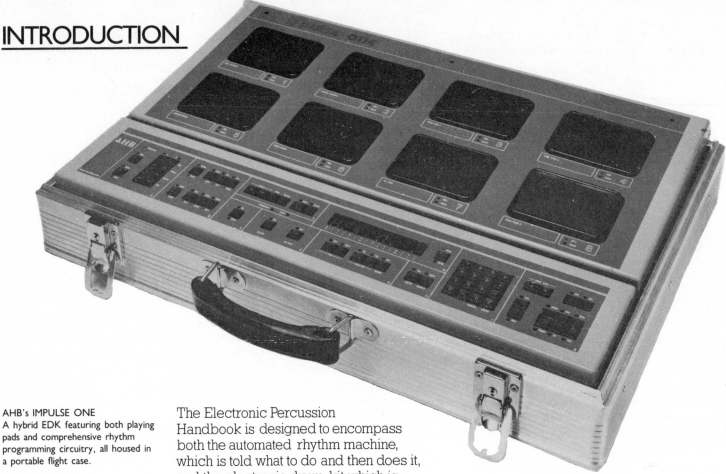

AHB's IMPULSE ONE
A hybrid EDK featuring both playing pads and comprehensive rhythm programming circuitry, all housed in a portable flight case.

YAMAHA MR-10
This low cost rhythm unit featured pre-set drum patterns. However, a set of pads on the front panel enabled the player to trigger the individual percussion voices, thus enabling him either to play real time patterns or to accompany those being produced automatically.

The Electronic Percussion Handbook is designed to encompass both the automated rhythm machine, which is told what to do and then does it, and the electronic drum kit which is 'played' in a roughly similar fashion to the conventional acoustic kit. The two instruments are obviously completely different in the way in which they are played. However, they are both designed for the same 'ultimate' purpose - to establish rhythm.

The rhythm unit has been criticised over the years for being clinical, lacking in feeling, dull, etc. In fact the rhythm unit has probably had more bad press than any form of musical instrument. And it is easy to see why. These devices first appeared in quantity during the 60s - primarily thanks to the advent of the transistor which made their manufacture commercially viable. They were preset devices - i.e. you would press a button and get a simple pattern, lasting one or two bars, continually repeating itself. They were primarily for pub/club pianists who needed a drum backing to enhance their performance - though the chronic inevitability of this repetitive, perfectly in-time beat added little. At this time the rhythm unit was little more than a glorified metronome.

The rhythm unit evolved out of all recognition thanks to one single development - programmability. Once people could make up their own rhythm patterns, and not have to rely on a host of foxtrot, waltz, and beguine preset rhythms, then interest in the product snowballed. Today's units resemble computers more than musical instruments, but their output is becoming less and less distinguishable from the real thing, especially in the hands of a good "user". The rhythm unit is primarily a 'remote' instrument, that is to say, it is told what to do (programmed) first, then once activated it performs its complete role, with little or no involvement from the musician. This is where the critics get their feet back in the door.

The electronic drum kit's history takes a completely different tack. The 60s saw the dawn of the age of amplified sound. Before, rock groups had been content to amplify just the guitars and piano/organ, and to leave the acoustic drum kit to fight its own way to the ears of the audience. But as time went by, it became increasingly apparent that the public wanted to hear more of the group, and less of the 'girls' in the front' screams. So increasingly powerful amplification rigs evolved until it became obvious that the only way the poor drummer could be heard was to "mic-up" his kit. This should have been the start of the electronic drum era. But it wasn't.

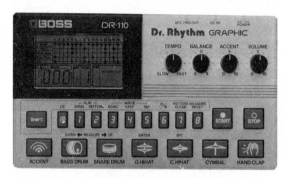

Drummers are a conservative bunch and particularly wary of anything new. Consequently, although it became necessary to double the amount of hardware surrounding them (mic stands etc.), they preferred to retain their existing acoustic instruments in preference to any electronic "gadget".

However, there came a point when technology had totally transformed the rest of the popular music industry - most notably the synthesizer had introduced a new timbral dimension. Devices then began to appear which made electronic sounds that were designed to supplement the traditional kit. Small flying-saucer type pads would be found nestled in amongst a set of tom-toms.

Eventually the first complete electronic drum kits came on the market, and in a similar way to which the synthesizer had transformed the keyboard market some ten years earlier, the electronic drum kit erupted on to the percussion world.

Electronic Percussion — WHY?

What are the advantages to the musician of using electronic percussion instruments?

Rhythm Units are:

a) compact.

b) can be effectively used by non-drummers.

c) do not require miking up.

d) compatible with other electronic instruments.

e) can have a very wide range of sounds,

both imitations of acoustic drums, or abstract sounds.

Electronic Kits are:

a) relatively compact and light.

b) do not require miking up.

c) can have a very wide range of sound, both imitations of acoustic drums, or abstract sounds.

d) can produce sounds of a similar 'feel' to acoustic drums.

Although they are different kinds of instruments, both these electronic percussion devices rely on a common factor - electronically derived drum sounds. So, after examining the basic principles of sound and electricity, this book will initially deal with the generation of these voices.

BOSS DR-110. A low cost analogue voice drum machine clearly illustrating the graphic window concept.

SIMMONS SDS-7 kit and brain.

CHAPTER I
SOUND AND
PERCUSSION

It is necessary, when considering any form of electronic musical instrument, to be aware of what exactly this device is striving to do. And so, like a writer who has to have some knowledge of the fundamentals of language in order to produce a literary work, anyone involved in the creation and use of sound, needs to know a little of the physics of the subject.

Sound is that sensation we experience when movement or vibrations in the air are detected by our ears. Our ears convert these vibrations into minute electrical pulses that are transmitted via our nervous system to the brain.

All the air around us is made up of billion upon billion of microscopic particles. You cannot see them because they are so small, but they are there. These particles make up the atmosphere of our planet. And it is these air particles that transmit the sound from its source to our ear.

How? By moving backward and forward so as to form denser and less dense variations in the air. It's a similar kind of phenomenon to the one you witness when you throw a stone into a pond. Where the stone hits the water a major disturbance takes place, and, if we were observing from directly above the pond, ripples would be seen to emanate from the centre at a fixed speed. These make what appear to be equally spaced concentric rings.

See *Fig. 1.01a*. Note that it is the waves that move out from the centre - not the actual particles of water. *Fig. 1.01b* shows the pond viewed as a cross section (i.e. as if you'd taken a vertical slice through the water and were looking edge on). At this point the stone hasn't hit the water, so the water level is flat. When the stone hits the water at point X *(Fig. 1.01c)* the water's surface becomes disturbed and regular ripples occur, moving away from the centre in all directions. These ripples equate to the concentric circles as shown in *Fig. 1.01a*. It can be seen that these ripples aren't composed of water that moves out from the centre, it is a vertical movement in the water that makes the ripples, and it is these waves that radiate from the disturbance.

Sound behaves in a similar fashion. When there's an explosion, say, sound waves travel out in all directions at a fixed speed. These sound waves consist of increases and decreases in the density of the air particles. As the waves radiate from the sound source, the air particles just increase and decrease in density. See *Fig. 1.02*.

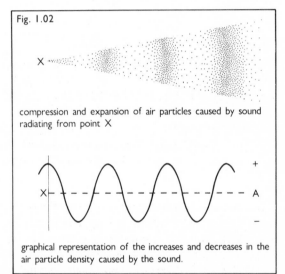

Fig. 1.02

X

compression and expansion of air particles caused by sound radiating from point X

graphical representation of the increases and decreases in the air particle density caused by the sound.

Remember, it is the air particles that transmit sounds from source to receiver.

You are probably familiar with the school-day experiment that proves the above statement. A ringing alarm clock is placed in a bell jar, then all the air is pumped out of the jar leaving a virtual vacuum. As the air is removed the sound becomes weaker and weaker until it is barely audible. As soon as air is restored to the jar, it is possible to hear the ringing again - thus proving that it is the air particles that transmit the sonic information.

The Three Elements of Sound

When we hear a sound we are experiencing a disturbance in the air particles of the atmosphere. This disturbance has three

Fig. 1.01

a)

bank   bank

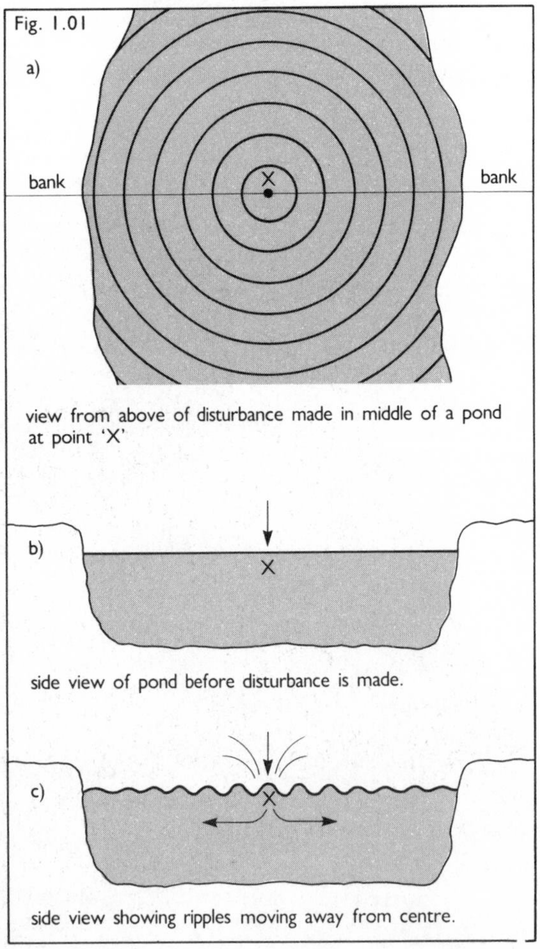

view from above of disturbance made in middle of a pond at point 'X'

b)

X

side view of pond before disturbance is made.

c)

X

side view showing ripples moving away from centre.

characteristics from which any sound can be defined: the pitch, the timbre (from the French word for tone colour), and the loudness (or amplitude).

Unfortunately, it's not quite that simple, as you might be listening to an orchestra, where the sound emanates from many sources and combines. Here it would be necessary to make a composite analysis. And it should also be stressed that these three parameters continually change throughout the duration of a sound. But if we can specify the pitch, timbre, and amplitude at every given instant in time we can create virtually any sound.

At first sight this seems as if the creation of a certain sound is going to be a long and laborious process — and it would be if we had to break the sound down into fractions of a second and specify each individual element. However, most electronic sound generators utilise shapes as a short cut in the definition of the changes of these three elements — and this greatly speeds things up.

Pitch

Pitch is the quality of a sound that makes it seem "high" or "low". If we hit a key at the bottom (left-hand) end of a piano, we generate a low-pitched sound, whilst the sound produced from the top end of a piano is considered to have a high pitch. Every key of the piano's keyboard produces a note of a slightly different pitch. A bass drum has a low pitch, whilst a small tom-tom has a high pitch.

Consider the example of the waves produced by the stone falling into the water. The circles spread out at a fixed rate, so each ripple is basically the same shape as the next. *Fig. 1.03* shows three such ripples, with the dotted line showing how the water looked before any disturbance. Now this

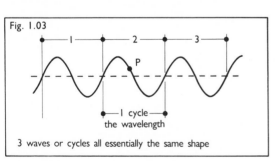

Fig. 1.03

1 cycle
the wavelength

3 waves or cycles all essentially the same shape

equates exactly to what happens when a sound is produced. The wave rises with an increase in air particle density and falls with a decrease, the dotted line being the air density when no sound is present. If we (the listener) were stationary these waves would pass by us at a certain speed (the speed of sound). This is approximately

330 metres per second.

Each wave repeats itself, so it should be possible to measure the length of the wave - the *wavelength*. So if our wave were 3 metres long, every second 110 of them would pass by us (the stationary observer). So if we considered a fixed point on the wave P, it would undergo 110 cycles every second. This is known as the *frequency* of the sound. The speed of sound is fixed, so the longer the waveform the lower the frequency (and hence pitch), and the shorter the waveform the higher the frequency (and pitch).

A simple formula exists that expresses this relationship:

FREQUENCY = speed of sound/wavelength

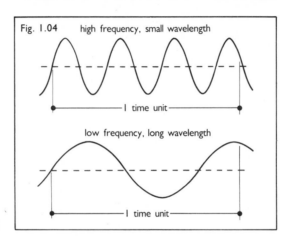

Fig. 1.04   high frequency, small wavelength

1 time unit

low frequency, long wavelength

1 time unit

Unpitched Sounds

Some percussive instruments, such as the cymbal, tambourine, gong, the 'snare' element of a snare drum, etc. have no specific pitch, i.e. their waveforms fail to exhibit a constantly repeating waveform. The simulation of unpitched sounds requires a slightly different technique to

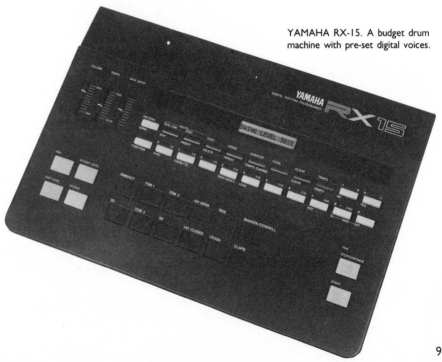

YAMAHA RX-15. A budget drum machine with pre-set digital voices.

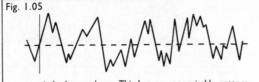

an un-pitched waveshape. This has no recognisable pattern, consequently it doesn't repeat itself and thus has no pitch.

that employed when producing pitched sounds.

Timbre

Timbre is the quality of a sound that enables the listener to distinguish it from another of the same pitch. The timbre (or tone colour) of a note depends on the actual shape of the waveform produced. If we return to our example of the stone being thrown in the water we can see how the compressions and rarefactions of the air determine the shape of the waveform produced. If this variation in density were less regular we might get something like that shown in *Fig. 1.06* If this sound had the same

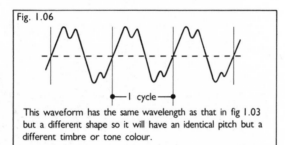

This waveform has the same wavelength as that in fig 1.03 but a different shape so it will have an identical pitch but a different timbre or tone colour.

wavelength as the sound in *Fig. 1.03* it would have the same pitch but it would sound different — it would have a brighter character to its sound. The shape of the

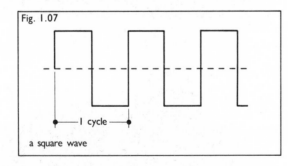

a square wave

waveform in *Fig. 1.03* is that of a sine wave, which is a pure mellow tone. The sharper the edges of a waveform the brighter that sound is perceived. Hard corners, such as that of a square wave *(Fig. 1.07)*, give the sound a considerably brighter quality.

Unlike pitch, there is no simple quantitative measurement of timbre. The only way to express this parameter is to describe the waveform produced. This is all very well for simple shapes, such as those we've already mentioned, but since just a small variation can make a considerable

difference to the timbre the ear perceives, then a more satisfactory method of describing this parameter is necessary.

A waveshape can be defined by means of a mathematical equation, but to most of us, this is more an academic exercise than of any practical use.

Loudness

The concept of loudness is, on the surface, a relatively simple one to grasp. Two sounds may have the same pitch and timbre, but it is possible still to distinguish between them if one sounds very loud, and the other very soft.

How does this relate to our compression and rarefaction of air particles concept?

Consider the example illustrated in *Fig. 1.08*. Here we have two states of existence:

i) Compression - whereby the density of the air particles abruptly becomes much greater than the average air density, and stays at this constant value for half the cycle.

ii) Rarefaction - when the density becomes less than the average, and there are less particles present per given area.

Now the loudness of the sound is governed by the relative amounts by which these densities vary. In *Fig. 1.08* we see three examples of this.

The wavelength and waveshapes remain

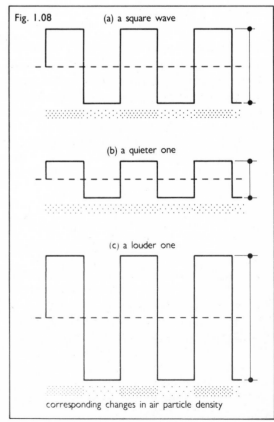

corresponding changes in air particle density

the same, just the variations in air densities are different, and the greater the difference the louder we perceive the sound. The greater the peaks and troughs the greater the amplitude, or loudness.

When listening to music, loudness isn't as simple as loud and soft. There's much more to it. In considering a sound the dynamics (or changes in loudness) are a vital aspect of the way in which we interpret the sound.

Sound Changes with Time

If you listen to the sound produced by almost any musical instrument you will be aware that these three parameters vary during the course of the note.

i) Loudness and Time: All sounds have what is known as a contour, or envelope, i.e. they have a starting point from which their loudness goes from nothing to a particular level. This level will probably change during the course of the sound, and there will eventually come a point when the loudness decreases and the sound ends. So the sound produced by playing a note on a piano (see *Fig. 1.09*)

However, a small low frequency variation in pitch will produce the effect known as "vibrato". Tuned percussive instruments sometimes start with an instantaneous rise in pitch which falls back as the note decays. In the case of tympani the pitch is often varied during the course of the sustained portion of the note.

YAMAHA RX-21. A low cost digital drum machine.

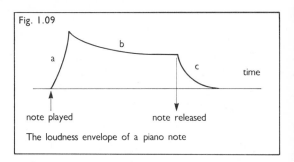

Fig. 1.09

The loudness envelope of a piano note

would have an envelope that started fairly abruptly as the hammer hit the strings (a), which would die away gradually as long as the note was held (b), and would then fall away sharply as the key was released and the dampers deadened the strings (c). The contour, or envelope, shapes the loudness of the note.

ii) Timbre and Time: The tone of most sounds changes during the course of the note. This is quite a complex phenomenon to illustrate, but we'll continue with the piano as our example. You can detect that the timbre of a note is much brighter when the key is struck; as the note dies away, the higher frequency elements of the sound tend to diminish even quicker, and the tone of the note becomes increasingly mellow.

iii) Pitch and Time: With most musical instruments the pitch remains relatively constant for the duration of the note.

The Human Ear and Sound

The three elements of sound described above are nice tidy concepts, all of which can be neatly evaluated mathematically. But then along we come with our ears, the receivers of the sound, and unfortunately, due to the limitations of the response of our ears, we have to make certain allowances when dealing with raw sound.

Our ears function rather like the speakers of a hi-fi system but in reverse. The compressions and rarefactions of any sound that reaches our ears cause a small membrane to vibrate back and forth. This vibration is detected by a series of small hairs contained within our inner ear. These generate a minute signal which is transmitted via our nervous system to the brain, and hey-presto! we hear noises. In essence it's

YAMAHA RX-21L. The "sister" to the RX-21, offering purely Latin percussive voices — not drums.

very simple, but like a hi-fi system our ears have limitations in the "quality" and range of sounds to which they can respond.

Our ears will react only to frequencies within a certain range, known as the Audible Frequency Spectrum. Why? Because the actual mechanism of the ear can operate only in a certain range. But even the best microphones cannot detect sounds as efficiently as the human ear.

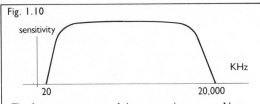

Fig. 1.10

The frequency response of the average human ear. Note that we cannot effectively detect pure frequencies below around 30 cycles per second but we could 'feel' them if they were sufficiently loud.

Generally speaking, the frequencies which a healthy young adult can detect range from between 18-25 Hz up to around 20,000 Hz, which in musical terms is around a ten octave span - wider than virtually all acoustic musical instruments, with the possible exception of the pipe organ. As with all parts of the body, age takes its toll, and the audible span of frequencies decreases, most notably towards the top end of the spectrum.

The Loudness of Percussive Sounds

The ear is capable of detecting an amazing range of sound levels. However, there is a lower limit to the volume of sound that the ear can detect - known as the threshold of human hearing. The other end of the scale is marked by the onslaught of pain. Sound pressure levels above this level can cause permanent damage to the ear, culminating in the perforation of the ear drum.

Percussive sounds, such as those produced from electronic percussion units, can be particularly dangerous at high sound levels, and, as they exist only for fractions of a second the warning symptoms of the reaching of the pain threshold can be almost instantly followed by damage to the ear drum. It is therefore advisable to take precautions if using electronic percussion instruments in conjunction with highly powered amplification systems.

Analogue and Digital

Analogue and Digital are two words that you will continue to encounter when dealing with any form of electronic musical instrumentation. They refer to the type of electronic circuitry being used: a) to produce a certain sound, and b) to control that sound once it has been produced.

Electricity

Electricity is simply the flow of microscopic charged particles, known as electrons, along a piece of conductive material such as wire. *Fig. 2.01* shows a domestic torch. The battery is the power source - it is charged so that when connected up, electrons will flow from one terminal to another.

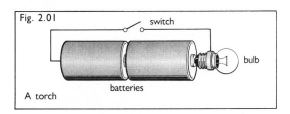

Fig. 2.01

switch

bulb

batteries

A torch

In our torch example, when the switch is closed (made) these electrons are free to move from one terminal of the battery to another. This they do with ease until they reach the bulb, where, because their passage is restricted, i.e. it is more difficult for them to flow through the element of the bulb, they have to work hard to get through. And in doing so heat is generated - this heats the element of the bulb up to such a point that it glows and gives off light.

An analogy would be you or me going for a walk from Point A to Point B; no problem along the flat, but if there's a wall in our way, we have to climb over it, expending a fair amount of energy — which results in our giving out heat.

It is this flow of electrons, or current as it is known, that we use to produce waveforms as described in Chapter 1. The flow of electrons in a conductor equates to the compression and rarefaction of the air particles. So imagine we have an electronic circuit that produces a flow, electrons that build rapidly to a high level, then all the electrons change direction and flow in the opposite direction, and then the cycle is repeated - you would get a waveform similar to that shown in *Fig. 2.02*. If you feed this signal to an amplifier, it will cause the diaphragm of the speaker to move in exactly the same way - out and back in etc. This will lead to compression and rarefaction of the air particles, and a sound corresponding to the shape of the original waveform will be produced.

AC and DC

The flow of electrons in a conductor is governed by a voltage. Small torch batteries may produce 1-1/2 to 9 volts. Our domestic mains supply provides 110/220/240 volts. The former provides a direct current, i.e. the flow of electrons is constant and in one direction, whilst the mains supply is known as an alternating current - the electrons are moving backward and forward (50 or 60 times a second).

In the context of electronics the terms "analogue" and "digital" relate to the way in which currents and voltages are manipulated. Anything that can continually vary is known as an analogue variable. Take as an example the domestic light bulb. At the entrance to each room is a switch which can be used to turn the light either on or off. This is a digital control signal as the state of the light bulb can be defined using the two numbers "0" and "1", "0" being "off", "1" being "on". If, however, we replaced our light switch with a dimmer switch, we could adjust the brilliance of the bulb to any level between "off" and "on" that we desired. Anything that can be continually varied is an analogue function.

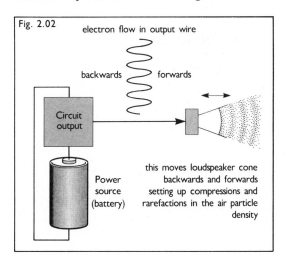

Fig. 2.02

electron flow in output wire

backwards   forwards

Circuit output

Power source (battery)

this moves loudspeaker cone backwards and forwards setting up compressions and rarefactions in the air particle density

The Digital Circuit

Being able to express the state of a light bulb as being either "on" or "off" doesn't seem to have particularly far reaching consequences in terms of electronic technology etc. But imagine an array of 200 × 500 such light bulbs. By simply saying which bulbs were "on" and which were "off" at any instant you could set the overall brightness produced by the array to any of 100,000 different levels; you could use the array on a large display screen and write messages; you could even draw pictures on the display and change which bulbs were "on" several times a second and get moving pictures. All this could be accomplished by using numbers (albeit

100,000 of them) each of which can only be "0" or "1". This is digital control.

Of course digital circuitry can be rationalised to more manageable proportions. Instead of having a number consisting of 100,000 binary digits (binary is a number system that uses only the numbers "0" and "1" as opposed to our ten digit system) you would generally have eight or sixteen binary digit words. To store greater amounts of information, these words (or bytes as they are known) change several hundred thousand times a second. *Fig. 2.03* shows how different values can be represented utilising 8-bit binary words.

Fig. 2.03	8 bit binary word		numerical equivalent
0 0 0 0 0 0 0 0	=	0	
0 0 0 0 0 0 0 1	=	1	
0 0 0 0 0 0 1 0	=	2	
0 0 0 0 0 0 1 1	=	3	
0 0 0 0 0 1 0 0	=	4	
0 0 0 0 1 0 0 0	=	8	
0 0 0 1 0 0 0 0	=	16	
0 0 1 0 0 0 0 0	=	32	
0 1 0 0 0 0 0 0	=	64	
1 0 0 0 0 0 0 0	=	128	
1 1 1 1 1 1 1 1	=	255	
1 0 1 0 1 1 0 1	=	173 (128 + 32 + 8 + 4 + 1)	

Digital Control

The 8-bit (12-bit or maybe 16-bit) binary word can be used for more than just representing a particular value. Imagine that you had a rhythm unit that had eight percussive voices. You could assign one bit of the word to each voice. See *Fig. 2.04*. Say that a bar of music lasted for 4 seconds and that the binary word changes four times a second, then each word could be

Fig. 2.04								
Time secs	Bass Drum	Snare Drum	Tom 1	Tom 2	Tom 3	HI HAT OPEN	HI HAT CLOSED	CYMBAL
0	1	0	0	0	0	0	1	0
¼	0	0	0	0	0	0	1	0
½	0	0	0	0	0	0	1	0
¾	0	0	0	0	0	0	1	0
1	0	1	0	0	0	0	1	0
1¼	0	0	0	0	0	0	1	0
1½	0	0	0	0	0	0	1	0
1¾	0	0	0	0	0	1	0	0
2	1	0	1	0	0	0	1	1
2¼	0	0	0	1	0	0	1	0
2½	0	0	1	0	0	0	1	0
2¾	0	0	0	1	0	0	1	0
3	0	1	0	0	1	0	1	0
3¼	0	0	0	0	0	0	1	0
3½	0	0	0	0	1	1	1	0
3¾	0	0	0	0	0	0	1	0
4—								

a new "word" is selected every ¼ second

every time a '1' appears that instrument sounds

used to trigger all the voices, and when a "1" appears on the digit being fed to a specific voice, then that voice sounds. This is, in simplistic terms, how a drum machine works. The binary words are held in a memory, and there can be any number of words to a pattern (depending on the time signature) though generally you will find 12, 16, 24, 32, 48, 64 words used. The tempo of the piece is governed simply by the rate at which the words change. This subject will be covered in more detail in Chapter 4.

The Analogue Circuit

Various electronic devices exist that enable us to control the flow of electrons in a circuit exactly as we wish. An oscillator is one such device that continually produces a waveform of a specific shape. The shape is a function of the various components used in the circuit. This is an analogue device because, throughout the circuit, currents and voltages are continually changing. The analogue circuit is the most commonly encountered device for simulating or synthesizing electronic percussive sounds. However, digital techniques, as we shall find, are employed for "sampled" drum sounds.

Percussive Voices

Nearly all of today's electronic percussion units utilise a microprocessor. This is an electronic device that acts like a small computer. In basic terms it performs relatively simple manipulative tasks on binary numbers. So it is a digital device. At the heart of any electronic percussion instrument are the instrument voices - the circuits that produce the sounds of the drums, cymbals etc. And these can usually be created in one of two ways - using digital or analogue circuitry.

If a digital circuit is used, the waveshape that represents the sound is stored as a series of numbers in the microprocessor's memory. This is illustrated in *Fig. 2.05*. A percussive sound contains frequencies throughout the audible frequency spectrum, so the waveshape representing the sound has to be capable of producing a sound of up to 15kHz - that's 15,000 cycles per second. In order to do this, the digital word that represents the value of this waveform at any given instant must change 30,000 times per second (a mathematical fact, the proof of which is beyond the scope of this book). So to get a good quality percussive voice we need to be able to store 30,000 8-bit words for one second of sound, although most percussive sounds (with the

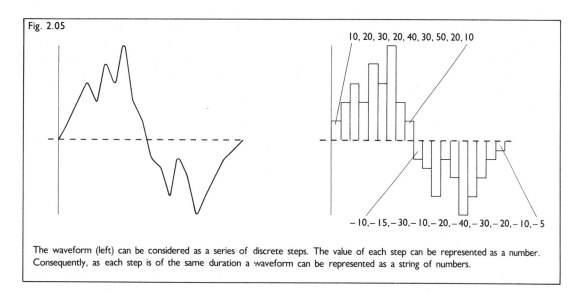

Fig. 2.05

10, 20, 30, 20, 40, 30, 50, 20, 10

−10, −15, −30, −10, −20, −40, −30, −20, −10, −5

The waveform (left) can be considered as a series of discrete steps. The value of each step can be represented as a number. Consequently, as each step is of the same duration a waveform can be represented as a string of numbers.

exception of cymbals) last for a fraction of a second. This is a lot of memory, and that's just for one sound.

An analogue circuit is the alternative. Here we have a more basic set of sub circuits that produce the sound, and unlike the digital circuit it is possible to vary certain parameters of the sound to tailor the particular drum sound. For a pitched percussive voice, an oscillator is used to produce a tone of a certain frequency. This is filtered to give the sound its specific tone, and the amplitude is then contoured to give the sound its dynamics. See *Fig. 2.06*. The analogue percussion unit, however, seems to be being phased out in preference to the clarity and realism that the digital generation system offers. We shall discuss the subject of percussion voices more thoroughly in the next chapter.

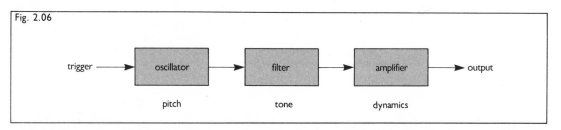

Fig. 2.06

trigger → oscillator → filter → amplifier → output

pitch | tone | dynamics

Roland CR-1000, a compact yet very versatile preset rhythm unit utilising digital voices.

CHAPTER 3
PERCUSSION VOICES

The percussion voices are the actual sound generators of the rhythm unit or electronic drum kit. Every time a particular beat of a rhythm is programmed, every time an electronic drum pad is struck, a trigger pulse is sent to a percussive voice and that voice produces the particular sound that it is designed to make.

Performance Parameters

Fig. 3.01 shows the way in which the percussive voices integrate into the whole picture of the rhythm machine and electronic drum kit. You can see that the final stages are very similar.

a rhythmic series of sounds to appear at the output.

The electronic drum kit is a somewhat more direct system. Trigger pulses are generated simply by the player hitting the pads with sticks. These pulses are fed to the respective voices.

In most electronic percussive devices the user has direct control over just two aspects of a particular voice.

a) When it sounds.
b) How loud it sounds.

The "when" is set by the point in time that a specific trigger pulse is sent to the voice. The "how loud" is determined by a

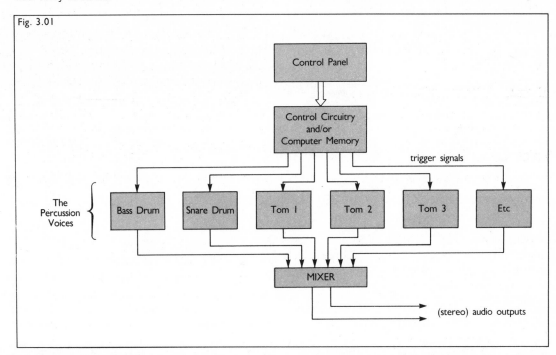

Fig. 3.01

When using a rhythm unit information is fed in via the control panel to the computer memory of the device where it is stored.

When the rhythm track is required the computer memory puts out relevant control pulses to the respective voice which in turn causes

separate control signal dependent, in the case of the electronic drum kit, on how hard the pad is hit. In some cases you will find that there is limited, if no, control over the loudness.

These two functions are the two main performance parameters, there are others which will be discussed more fully in the chapters dealing specifically with the control mechanism of rhythm units and electronic kits.

So in the simplest case a percussive voice will receive just "note-on" information - i.e. when to sound. It might also receive some dynamic information which can be interpreted in several different ways.

Voices

The rôle of the electronic percussion voice is twofold. It is imitative - to recreate the sound and character of an acoustic kit; or it is abstract - the sounds generated bearing no relation to those produced by the acoustic namesake.

The voices 1 to 5 (below) are normally to be found on a rhythm unit:

1) Snare Drum.
2) Bass Drum.
3) Tom Tom (two or more).
4) Hi-Hat (open and closed).
5) Cymbal (crash and ride).
6) Cowbell.
7) Handclaps.
8) Rim shot.
9) Tambourine.
10) Claves

Voices 6-10 are less frequently encountered, although most rhythm units will feature some of them. Some more elaborate machines will feature yet more exotic sounds such as:

11) Woodblock
12) Cabasa
13) Gong
14) Shaker
15) Timpani

Voice Generation

There are two distinct ways in which a voice produces a sound:

1) *Analogue:* The term "analogue" as mentioned on page 14 refers to a continually varying medium, in this case voltage. By using synthesizer techniques, and circuits such as oscillators, filters, and envelope shapers, we can synthesize specific percussive sounds. This is the more traditional form of voice synthesis - used both in the original rhythm units and, in hybrid formats, in most electronic kits.

2) *Digital:* Digitally generated percussion voicings are generally recordings of real drum sounds, i.e. when the voice is triggered the pre-recorded sound of that particular drum is replayed. Of course these "recordings" of digital voices aren't made on tape - they are stored in the electronic memories in the form of a string of numbers. When the voice is triggered these numbers are turned into an analogue signal (see page 13/14).

Both systems have their inherent advantages and disadvantages which will become increasingly apparent as we look in greater detail at these two voicing techniques.

Analogue Voicing

There are two kinds of analogue percussive voice, the preset and the variable. A preset voice is set up in the factory and you can alter virtually none of its characteristics. The way in which these

SIMMONS SDS-1. A single electronic drum which can be used either in conjunction with an electronic kit or as an add on to an acoustic kit.

sounds are constructed varies from machine to machine, and from voice to voice, and knowledge of how these preset voices are created is of little use to the end user. However, when considering percussive voices that can be user-programmed, and especially when these voices are to be employed with an electronic drum kit, it is necessary to know exactly what is happening in the sound creation process in order that a drummer may tailor the sound to fit the style and requirements of his playing.

There is generally a basic format which is adopted by most manufacturers. Those who feel they don't need to know about analogue percussive sound creation should proceed to the next section.

You should now be familiar with the concept of the three elements of sound, Pitch, Timbre and Loudness. By specifying these three parameters you can define virtually any sound. This is primarily synthesizer technology, but when producing a percussive sound there is one distinct difference - there is no Sustain. When you play a keyboard such as a synthesizer you depress the note, hold it down for a particular length of time, then release it. With drums it's not quite like that. The hitting of a drum is a "one-off" - you hit the drum with the stick and once that has been done, you then have virtually no control over the ensuing sound. This can be depicted diagrammatically (*Fig. 3.03*). The keyboard note has an ON time (the sustain period), whilst the drum is an

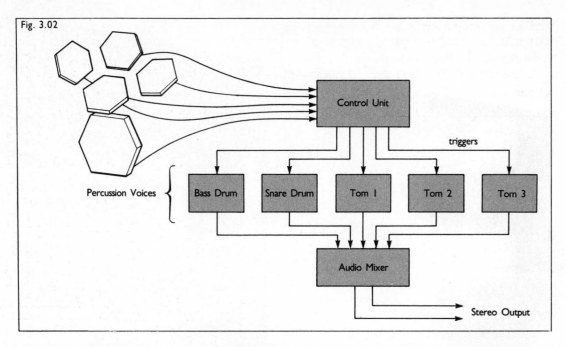

Fig. 3.02

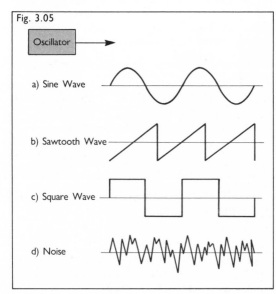

Fig. 3.03

instantaneous event. As we shall see, this is reflected in the electronic circuitry of the percussion voice.

Fig. 3.04 shows a block diagram of a simple voice:

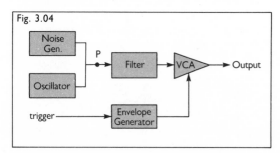

Fig. 3.04

The Oscillator: If we are striving to create a pitched sound such as a tom-tom, bass, or snare drum, then the oscillator is the starting point. The speed (frequency) at which it runs determines the pitch of the sound. And the way in which it oscillates, i.e. the waveform produced by the oscillator, gives the basic tone of the sound. If the sound required is an unpitched one (e.g. a cymbal), then a noise source of some kind is generally employed. *Fig. 3.05* shows three typical waveforms produced by an oscillator:

a) a sine wave, is a pure mellow tone, good for bass drum sounds.
b) a sawtooth wave, which is more brassy in character.

c) a square wave, a hollow tone.

b) and c) require a degree of filtering (see next page) in order to derive useful percussive sounds.

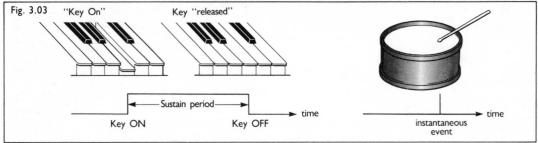

Fig. 3.05

The Noise Generator: This is a form of oscillator, but one that produces a random collection of oscillations such that its overall output has no vestige of pitch. How can this be? Consider the sound of a cymbal - unlike a drum, it has no specific pitch. White noise is similar in terms of sound output, though the hiss produced by a

VHF radio when it isn't tuned to any particular station is a closer approximation to the sound of white noise.

So the oscillator is used as a basis for

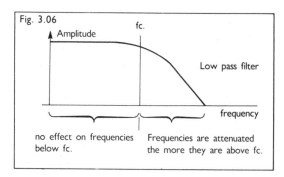

tuned percussion sounds and the white noise generator for un-pitched voices. At this stage it should be made clear that the signal produced by the oscillator/noise generator (point P on *Fig. 3.04*) is a constant drone (we will discuss oscillator modulation later). There is no concept of a beginning and ending to a sound, this comes later. There is an analogy here to the bulb of a movie projector - it is on all the time, it's

Fig. 3.06

Amplitude

fc.

Low pass filter

frequency

no effect on frequencies below fc.

Frequencies are attenuated the more they are above fc.

what happens between it and the screen that determines the intensity and nature of the image.

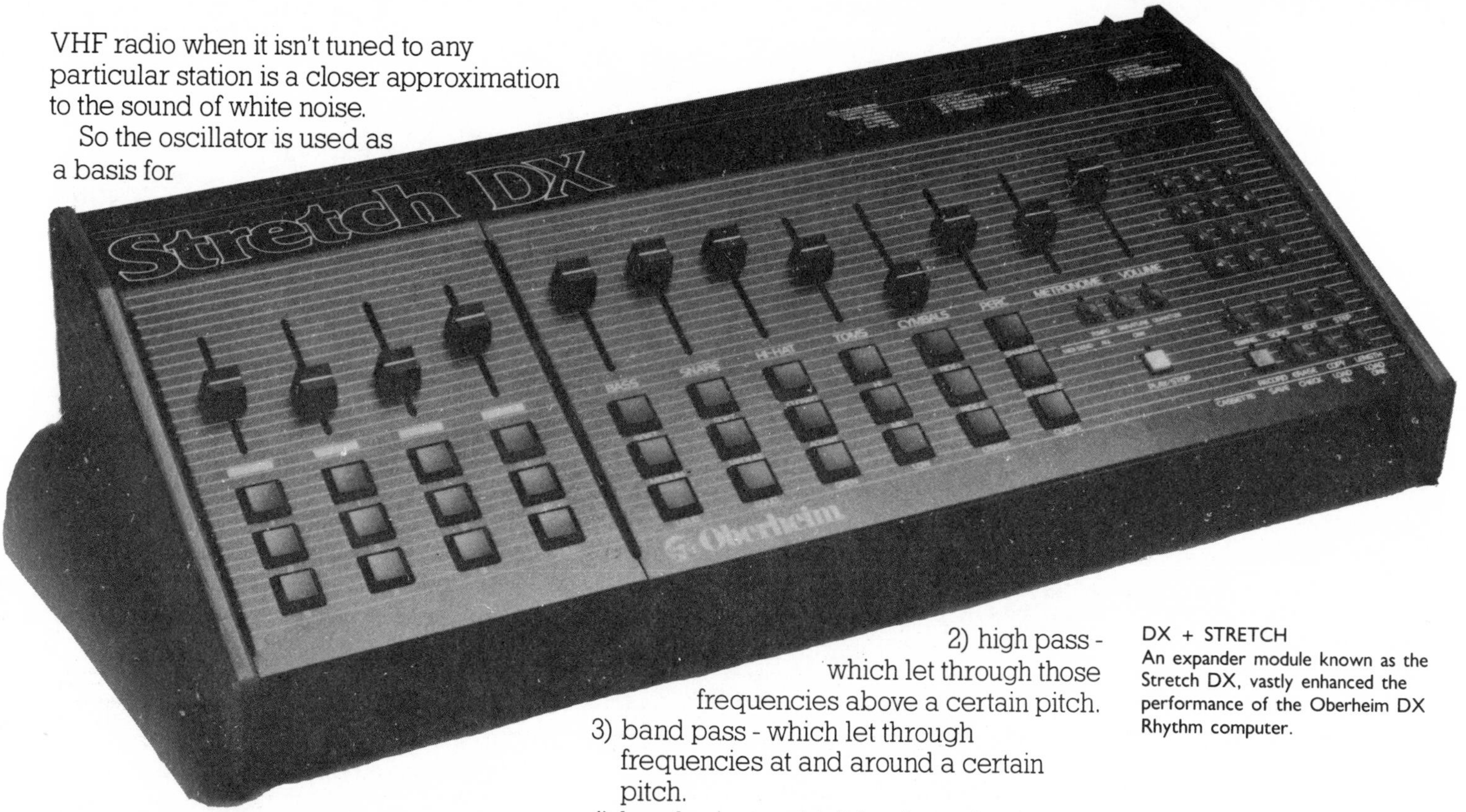

The Filter: The filter used in electronic percussion voices is just a glorified tone control. It removes those parts of the oscillator/noise generator's signal that aren't required leaving, hopefully, a tone with the desired timbre. There are many different forms of filter used in electronic percussion units, varying from the simple brilliance control to complex multi-state filters.

There are four common types of filter:
1) low pass - which let through those frequencies below a certain pitch.

2) high pass - which let through those frequencies above a certain pitch.
3) band pass - which let through frequencies at and around a certain pitch.
4) band reject - which let through only those frequencies below and above a certain pitch.

But the most commonly used is the low pass filter. In *Fig. 3.06* it can be seen that the filter has little or no effect on the sound below a certain frequency (the cut-off frequency), but that the filter rapidly attenuates those parts of the signal that are pitched above the cut-off point. Thus,

Fig. 3.07

trigger pulse

time

having been processed by a low pass filter, the sound becomes more mellow and less bright than the original. We will look at more aspects of the filter shortly.

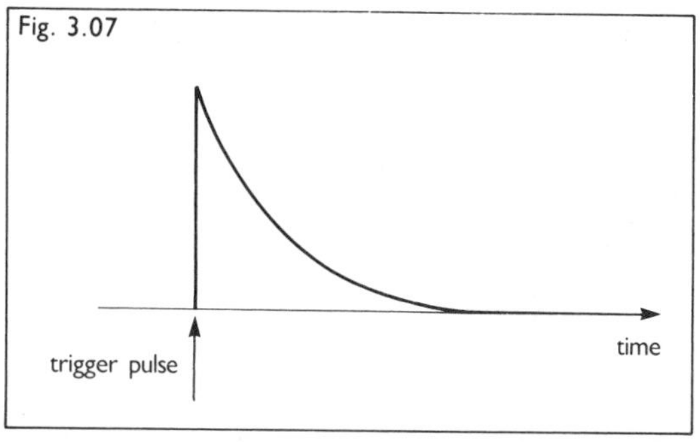

The Amplifier and Envelope Generator

Were the output of the filter to be fed to an amplifier a constant drone would still be heard; it is therefore necessary to give the sound a contour, i.e. a start and a finish.

The filtered sound is fed to a device which, for ease, we will consider to be a Voltage Controlled Amplifier (VCA). This also accepts a control signal from a device known as an envelope generator, and amplifies or attenuates the loudness of the

DX + STRETCH
An expander module known as the Stretch DX, vastly enhanced the performance of the Oberheim DX Rhythm computer.

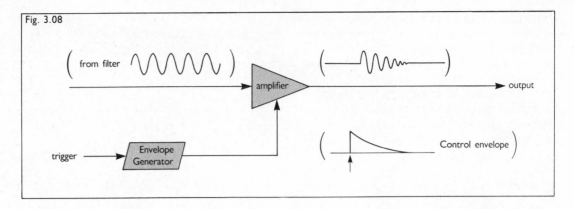

Fig. 3.08

'drone' in proportion to the size and shape of this envelope.

It is the envelope that receives the trigger information, be it from the central control of the rhythm unit or via the pad of an electronic drum kit. Upon receipt of this "Go" pulse, a single waveform like that shown in *Fig. 3.08* is produced. As can be seen, the instant the trigger pulse is received the envelope rises to a maximum level, and then slowly falls back to its initial position. The time it takes to return to this state is known as the decay time. This parameter is usually a variable that can be set up by the player.

This envelope is then fed to the Voltage Controlled Amplifier. The continually sounding audio input from the filter is thus shaped by this control envelope. The final sound adopts changes in volume directly in accordance with the envelope, thus when the envelope is at a low level awaiting a trigger signal, the VCA attenuates the signal so that no sound can be heard. *Fig. 3.08*.

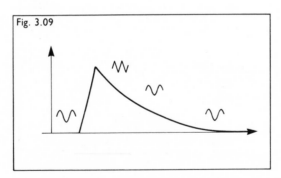

Fig. 3.09

These are the fundamental circuit elements that go to make up an analogue voice, but in the more elaborate instruments a far more complex set-up is employed.

Modulation

Sound is constantly changing with time. We've seen how the loudness of a sound can be automatically shaped using an envelope generator. But to get the most out of a sound-producing device it is also necessary to be able to have the pitch and the timbre varying over the course of the

note. This automatic control over the fundamental elements of the sound is called Modulation. There are two distinct types - periodic and aperiodic.

Periodic modulation is the repetitive variation of the parameter, whilst aperiodic modulation, like the application of the control envelope to the VCA, is a one-off operation. Something has to be re-triggered in order for the event to occur again.

A periodic and an aperiodic event could be the firing of a machine gun and an ordinary gun respectively. Pull the trigger of a machine gun and the bullets keep being fired until the trigger is released - a periodic event; pull the trigger of an ordinary gun and a single bullet is sent flying - to send another, the trigger has to be pulled again.

Aperiodic Modulation of the Filter

If you listen to the timbre of a percussive sound such as a cymbal you will notice that the timbre seems much brighter the instant that it is struck. This holds true with a wide range of acoustic sounds as more harmonics are produced at that initial instant. This is electronically simulated by using an envelope (aperiodic) waveform to alter the cut-off frequency of a low pass filter *(Fig. 3.09)*. A low pass filter is chosen because as the cut-off frequency rises with the envelope it allows more of the signal to pass - as the envelope falls, so these higher frequency components of the sound are eliminated and the timbre of the sound mellows.

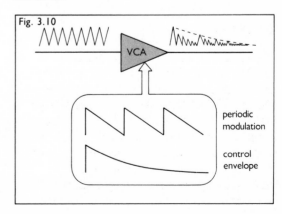

Fig. 3.10

Aperiodic Modulation of the Oscillator

Consider what happens when you hit a tom tom or a tympani. Both drums are tuned, i.e. they have a definite pitch which is dependent on various factors such as the size of the drum and the tensioning of the skin over the head. When played, their pitch tends to rise slightly then fall back a little. This can be simulated electronically by using an envelope to modulate the frequency of the oscillator. So as the voice is triggered the envelope 'fires', feeding a small control signal to the filter which rises in pitch to match the shape of the envelope. Obviously, the greater the control signal the greater the effect on the pitch of the sound.

Periodic Modulation: The low frequency oscillator could also be used to apply a constantly repeating modulation to any of the three elements of pitch, timbre, and loudness. The effect of such modulation varies depending on the type of waveform used. When considering percussion synthesis, the most common form of periodic modulation is amplitude related. By applying a ramp wave and a control envelope to the voltage controlled amplifier it is possible to produce echo-like effects (Fig. 3.10).

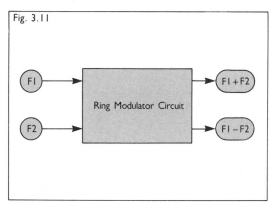

Fig. 3.11

Periodic modulation of the filter is very rarely used; while periodic modulation of the oscillator results in vibrato or trill effects, which are more commonly utilised in the more traditional world of music synthesis.

Ring Modulation

The Ring Modulation is a rather useful method of creating sounds that are very rich in harmonics, especially bell-like sounds. Unlike the previously discussed methods of modulation which use an audio pitch with a control waveform, this process requires two oscillators normally running at frequencies within the audible frequency spectrum. The two signals are fed into this circuit and at the output two

new signals are produced - one running at the arithmetical sum of the two frequencies, the other at the arithmetical difference (Fig. 3.11). Thus:

IN : F1, F2
OUT : (F1+F2), (F1−F2).

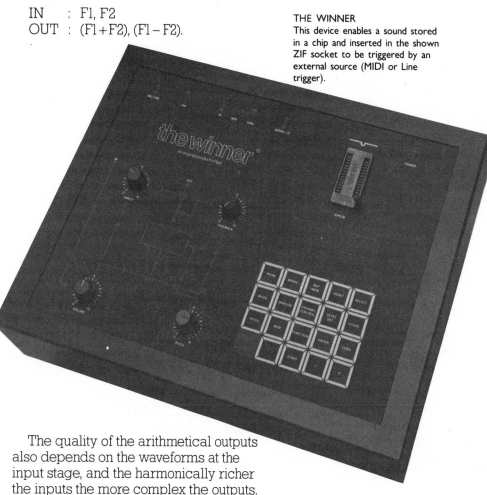

THE WINNER
This device enables a sound stored in a chip and inserted in the shown ZIF socket to be triggered by an external source (MIDI or Line trigger).

The quality of the arithmetical outputs also depends on the waveforms at the input stage, and the harmonically richer the inputs the more complex the outputs. The result is a waveform that can be very harsh and metallic sounding - which is ideal for many types of percussive voicings - especially cymbals and bells.

Fig. 3.12

Cross Modulation

This is a type of periodic frequency modulation, only with both oscillators generally running at frequencies in the audio spectrum. Again the result is a waveform that is harmonically very rich, but it doesn't have the same metallic characteristics as the ring modulated Waveform (Fig. 3.12).

Clicks

When a drum stick strikes the head of a drum, there is invariably an initial sound of some sort produced before the body of the drum has a chance to impart its own characteristic sound. Electronically this is generated using a very short burst of noise and is generally added to the final stage of the sound. The player usually has control over just the amplitude of the click, and occasionally over the decay time.

Summary

Analogue percussion voices are generated in a wide variety of ways - the above is a formulated version of the type of parameters you will come across when programming your own sounds. To simplify matters *Fig. 3.13* shows a typical voice of which you might have control over the following:

Signal Generators

Pitch.
Pitch Bend (envelope modulation of pitch).
Pitch Modulation.

Noise.
Balance (between noise and oscillator levels).
Click.

Timbre.

Filter Frequency.
Filter Bend (envelope modulation of filter frequency).
Filter Resonance.

Amplitude

Decay (envelope modulation of amplitude).
Volume.

LFO Modulation

Speed.
Shape.

If you are familiar with these parameters you should be able to create your own percussive voices with relative ease.

Experimentation is of course the best way to develop such programming skills.

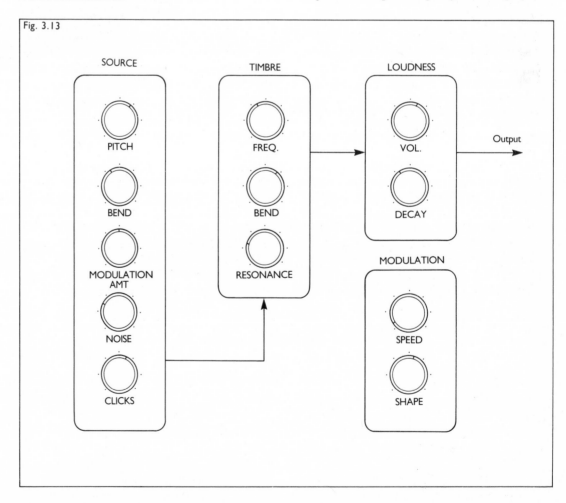

Fig. 3.13

SOURCE — PITCH, BEND, MODULATION AMT, NOISE, CLICKS
TIMBRE — FREQ., BEND, RESONANCE
LOUDNESS — VOL., DECAY
MODULATION — SPEED, SHAPE
Output

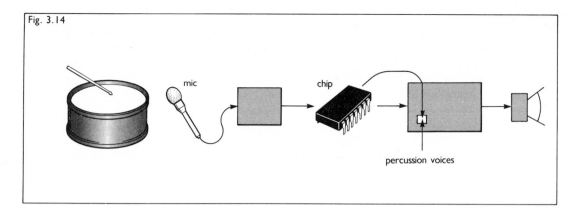

Fig. 3.14

mic

chip

percussion voices

Digital Voices

Digital voices are non-creative, that is to say, unlike analogue voices where the actual voice is actively being generated within the circuit, a digital voice is simply a recreation of a "pre-recorded" sound, but instead of using tape to store the sound an electronic memory is utilised. Digital voices are far less flexible than analogue ones because you cannot "get into" the sound to manipulate the various parameters.

The best way to explain this system is with a practical example. Consider a snare drum sound. At the manufacturing stage, you need to start with the sound you finally want to be produced by the rhythm unit. This sound is then translated into a series of numbers (see section 2 page 14) which are stored in a memory chip. The chip is then installed in a rhythm unit or electronic kit. When the voice is triggered the string of numbers is recalled from the chip memory and reassembled into an audio signal of the original snare sound.

As you can see, as this is simply a replay system there is little scope for modifying the actual character of the sound. But there are a couple of ways in which the sound can be modified, and again these facilities are generally to be found on electronic drum kits - the voices of rhythm units are usually preset.

1) Pitch: If you have a tape recording of a sound you can vary its pitch by adjusting the tape speed. The faster the tape is played the higher the pitch. The same principles operate when using digital sounds. By increasing the rate at which the numbers that make up digital sound are translated into an audio signal (the clock rate), the pitch of the sound can be increased. Naturally, if you slow down this rate the pitch falls. There is a "side effect". By replaying the sound at a faster rate you are using up all the digital information much quicker, consequently the sound will not last so long.

2) Reverse: The percussive sound is stored as a group of numbers and although there is little that can be done to change the timbral make-up of the sound, it is possible to read the numbers in different ways, and instead of starting at the beginning we can read the numbers backwards thus starting with the end of the sound. So as shown in *Fig. 3.15*, the contour of a cymbal envelope is reversed with the sound gradually building up then cutting off sharply. The reverse effect may not be particularly useful - it certainly transforms an authentic sounding percussive voice into a purely abstract sound - but it offers the user a wider range of unusual sounds from a percussion instrument.

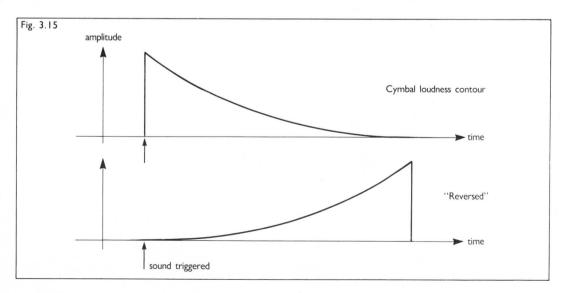

Fig. 3.15

amplitude

Cymbal loudness contour

time

"Reversed"

time

sound triggered

Digital/Analogue Hybrids

Some percussive sounds, such as cymbals, have a fairly long duration lasting for several seconds. The memory chips used to store these sounds are extremely expensive, consequently any way in which less memory can be used to save a sound helps to keep costs down. One way in which this can be achieved is 'looping'. *Fig. 3.16a* represents a complete cymbal voicing. The timbre of this sound varies little over the initial period. A digital recording of the sound can be made, but this will use a lot of memory as the sound lasts for several seconds. So take a portion of the sound (shaded). Here we have a small part of the cymbal sound, and if we loop (repeat over and over) this section we should have something approximating to the continuous sound of a cymbal. *Fig. 3.16b.*

Obviously a cymbal drone of this nature is of little use, so we have to shape the sound using analogue circuitry - a VCA and an Envelope Generator. The latter is set up to produce an envelope with the same shape as that of the original cymbal contour *(Fig. 3.16c)*. Thus we get a sound as depicted in *Fig. 3.16d* which has a very similar sound to the original, but which uses very little memory.

Looping is an extremely useful facility and is discussed further in the section on Sampling.

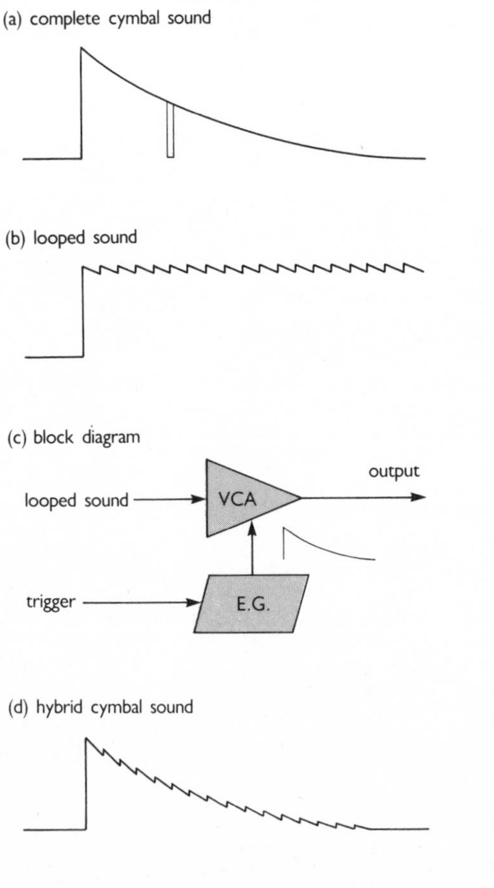

The marriage of digital and analogue circuitry offers a way to achieve the best results when programming percussive voices. Again, if the voicing is preset, a straight sample is often best as there is no requirement to "get inside" the sound. But the electronic drum kit has to be more flexible, consequently the voices do have to offer the player considerable scope to create his own particular sounds. *Fig. 3.17* depicts a particularly comprehensive digital/analogue voice.

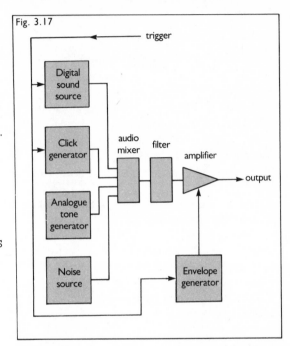

Fig. 3.17

Sampling

One kind of digital voice features "sampling". As shown, digital voices aren't particularly flexible, therefore in order to make the most of the particular percussion unit being employed it is extremely useful to be able to load the instrument with your own voices, i.e. to load and use recordings you've made of percussion sounds, rather than to rely on those loaded into the machine at the factory. A percussion unit that offers this facility earns the tag of "sampler".

The concept of sampling percussion voices sounds an ideal one - load up a drum machine with all your favourite sounds and you've got everything you need in an electronic percussion device. But that's not the case. Again, as with the straight factory programmed digital sounds you have little control over the sound once it has been sampled. Consider what happens when you strike a snare drum. The sound isn't exactly the same every time you strike the head. The sound which is heard depends primarily on:

i) the force with which you strike the skin.
ii) which part of the drum you strike.
iii) what type of stick you are using.

Fig. 3.16

(a) complete cymbal sound

(b) looped sound

(c) block diagram

looped sound → VCA → output

trigger → E.G.

(d) hybrid cymbal sound

These factors mainly help to determine the loudness and timbre of the sound, the pitch is only slightly affected by them. So although you may have sampled a great snare sound, you will have a fixed voice held in the instrument's memory. The volume of the sound can be controlled using analogue circuitry as per *Fig. 3.08*, but the timbral characteristics will always be as per the sample (unless sophisticated analogue filtering is employed).

Memory Chips

When dealing with digital and sampling circuitry, the key element in the system is memory. It is vital to be able to store the data that makes up a sound in some form of memory device. The most commonly used memory devices are chips - i.e. small electronic circuits capable of storing strings of numbers which represent, in this case, the voicing information. *Fig. 3.18* shows a typical memory chip which is singularly unexciting in terms of appearance.

There are various types of memory chips, all of which have the same basic purpose (storing information) but which function in different ways.

The most commonly used terms are ROMs and RAMs. An analogy can be made between ROMs/RAMs and records/tapes. A ROM, like a record, contains fixed information - you cannot alter it (save by scratching the record), whereas a RAM, like an audio cassette, can be used to store any information you like - this information can be erased and altered as necessary.

When a sound is sampled a large amount of Random Access Memory (RAM) is employed. Preset digital sounds would be stored in Read Only Memory (ROM).

Unfortunately, when you load information (in the form of a string of numbers) into a RAM it remains there only so long as the power continues to be applied to the circuit. So it is necessary to have some kind of back-up power supply (e.g. a tiny battery)

to keep the RAM working when the main body of the instrument is switched off. ROMs don't suffer from this problem because they have had information "blown" into them at the factory, i.e. the data is permanently etched into them.

Various derivatives of the ROM/RAM family exist, and it is as well to know what they are as they will undoubtedly be encountered when utilising digital percussion units.

EPROMs. An erasable and programmable ROM *(Fig. 3.19)*. Although the data has been 'permanently' loaded into the memory at the manufacturing

Fig. 3.18

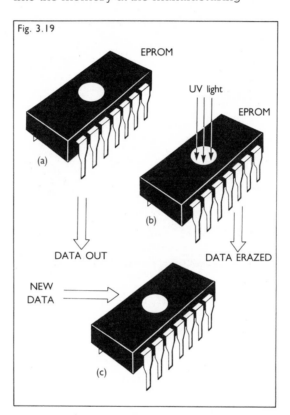

Fig. 3.19

EPROM

UV light

EPROM

(a)

(b)

DATA OUT

DATA ERAZED

NEW DATA

(c)

stage, it can be wiped out and the chip used to store a new set of data. The erasing procedure normally consists of exposing the chip to ultra-violet (UV) light. As you can see from the figure, the chip has a small window on its top. The ultra-violet light permeates this window and clears the chip of any data. Many drum

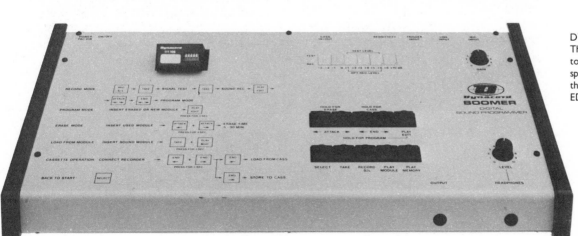

DYNACORD SOUND SAMPLER
This Sound Sampler enables the user to create digital recordings of specific drum sounds which could then be integrated into his EDK/drum machine.

machines and electronic kits are fitted with what are known as ZIF (Zero Insertion Force) sockets - see *Fig. 3.20*. These allow for the fast interchange of EPROMs so it is possible to change one or more voices of a digital percussion unit quickly and easily. A device known as an EPROM blower (see below) is used to sample sounds, put them into a digital format and then permanently store them in an EPROM memory.

EEPROM: An Electronically Erasable ROM. These devices, which are considerably more expensive than EPROMs, actually equate to a RAM, but need no battery back-up. Instead of being wiped by exposure to UV light the data stored within an EEPROM is erased by means of an electrical control signal. Therefore when plugged into a piece of equipment the data can be altered, but when power is removed the data remains intact.

Fig. 3.20

Fig. 3.21

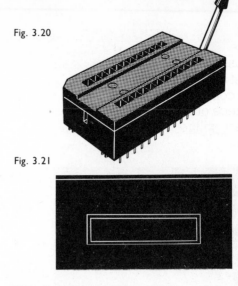

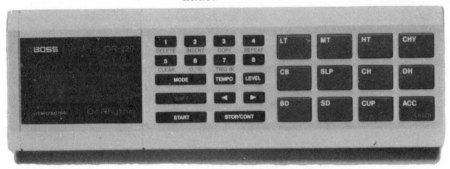

BOSS DR-220
A compact rhythm unit based on the popular format of the DR-110, but utilising digitally encoded percussion voices.

Opening up an instrument to change a memory chip is potentially hazardous. Consequently manufacturers often fit their memory chips into a cartridge (*Fig. 3.21*) which plugs into a socket on the exterior of the instrument. This is far more acceptable to the majority of players - cartridges are far more sturdy and resilient to damage, and they are also quicker and easier to use.

EPROM BLOWER (EPB)

The EPROM blower is used by a player who wants to sample a sound and use it as a source sound for his drum machine/ electronic kit. In most cases there is little interplay between manufacturing companies - i.e. if you are using a Simmons electronic drum kit, you need to blow your EPROMs with a Simmons EPROM blower.

Generally the EPB will have its own internal memory (RAM). The sound to be sampled is fed into the unit, either via a microphone or a line input, and the levels adjusted accordingly. The EPB will detect the onset of the sound and instantaneously translate the audio signal into a chain of digital numbers which it stores in its on-board RAM. You can now replay and hear this sound by hitting a button on the panel of the EPB. If the recording is acceptable, the data is then blown into the EPROM which has been inserted into a ZIF socket on the top of the unit. Once blown the data is permanently stored within the EPROM which can then be inserted into the relevant drum machine or electronic kit.

SIMMONS EPROM BLOWER.
Electronic memory chips are inserted in the ZIF socket (centre), and sounds of around a second's duration can be loaded into this chip as a means of permanent storage; the chip is then used in conjunction with an electronic drum kit's brain.

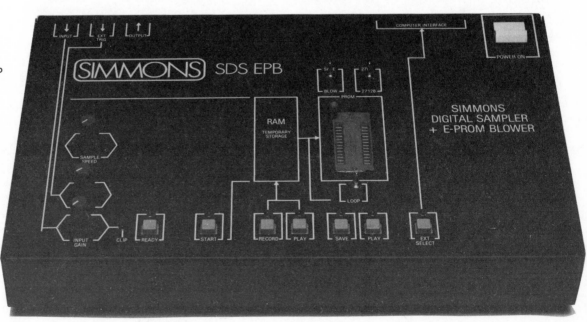

There are various names given to this device - drum machine, rhythm unit, percussion computer, beat box, or in fact almost any permutations thereof. The basic concept behind this device is that it is a piece of equipment which, upon request, will replay a pre-programmed rhythm pattern or track.

units were produced which would produce certain preset rhythm patterns upon request. These devices were completely electronic and had to be plugged into an amplifier in order for any sound to be heard. They were primarily designed for the piano player who wanted a rhythmic accompaniment, and they found great

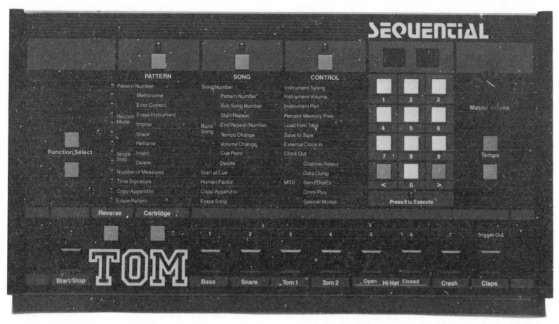

SEQUENTIAL TOM. A versatile digital drum machine with unique digital voice manipulation facilities.

The roots of the drum machine lie as far back as the fairground organ of the late 19th and early 20th century. These spectacular devices consisted of sets of band instruments played automatically by a pneumatic system - i.e. steam or air - to control the various elements. The tune was pre-programmed in a similar fashion to the rolls used to drive the pianola, but with many different instruments being controlled. Naturally, such fairground music required some form of rhythm and consequently drums and cymbals were also driven. By changing the "roll" the tune to be played could naturally be changed.

The 'domestic' organ appeared in the 1930s, but it didn't really start to become a serious instrument for the home until the early 1960s. With advanced electronic circuitry, the home organ gave the musician the ability to produce a variety of different sounds, but it was when manufacturers started incorporating rhythm units into their organs that these instruments became most popular. Now the one-man musician at home, could create a complete musical arrangement - the home organ with its rhythm unit was capable of producing good quality versions (assuming the player had the ability) of most of the day's popular music.

The success that this device brought to the home organ inspired manufacturers to release the rhythm unit section of the home organ on its own. And so separate

popularity in pubs and clubs where the percussion backing considerably enhanced a one-man performance.

An acoustic drum kit is an extremely large and inconvenient musical instrument. Consequently these compact units, although nowhere replacing the presence and feel of the drummer, were an extremely attractive alternative.

From those days on the drum machine has become increasingly advanced, and its power to replace the conventional kit that much greater. In quite a few cases, especially when it comes to popular music, one would be hard pressed to tell whether a drum machine was being used or whether it's "the real thing".

We will look more closely at some of the major instruments in the drum machines' history towards the end of this chapter.

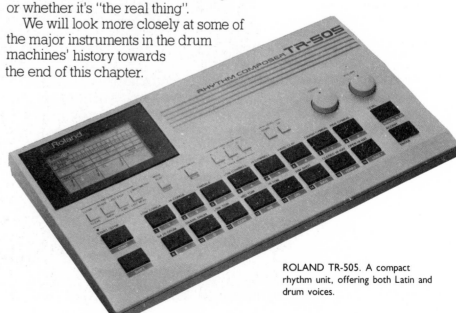

ROLAND TR-505. A compact rhythm unit, offering both Latin and drum voices.

The Drum Machine Modules

A drum machine consists of two distinct "modules" - i) the controller and ii) the voices. We have looked in depth at percussion voices in the previous chapter, but it is the way in which these voices are triggered that is important when considering the drum machine, so we will concentrate on the former.

The Controller

The controller section of a drum machine is simply a device that dictates when things will happen.

There are two modes in which a rhythm unit operates:

Programming Mode entails telling the rhythm unit what you want it to do.

Performance Mode is when, upon activation (normally by the pressing of a Start button), it does it.

Today's drum machines are nearly all programmable. However, in the early days, before these units realised their full potential, they were capable of playing only popular, simple rhythm figures (such as Waltz, Foxtrot, Bossa Nova etc.) that had been pre-programmed at the manufacturing stage. So with these instruments the user's contribution during the programming mode simply involved the selection of a particular preset pattern. Upon hitting the Start button, the controller thus sent trigger pulses to the various voices as and when each had to sound. The pattern continued to repeat itself until the Stop button was pressed.

YAMAHA RX-11 is a powerful digital rhythm unit, offering separate audio outputs for the percussion voices.

But with programmable rhythm units the story is considerably more involved.

Patterns, Songs and Chains

Before getting involved with the in-depth working and programming of the drum machine, there are three important terms to consider.

PATTERN - a drum pattern is a rhythmic phrase usually lasting between 1 and 4 bars.

SONG - in the context of the rhythm unit a "song" is a series of patterns running sequentially to form the rhythm track to a section of music. It doesn't necessarily mean the complete rhythmic track to an entire piece - if the rhythm unit has a CHAIN facility, it would more often than not be just a verse or a chorus to a song. So, in this instance, say you were composing the rhythm track to a 3 minute pop song, the format of the chorus might run something like:

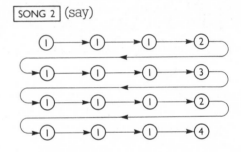

A different "song" (say Song 1) might be used for the verse with other "songs" used to provide the rhythmic accompaniment for the introduction, "middle-8" and end.

CHAIN - a chain is a string of "songs" that run sequentially. If, as referred to above, we were using "songs" as verses and choruses, then the Chain would actually equate to the complete rhythm track of a

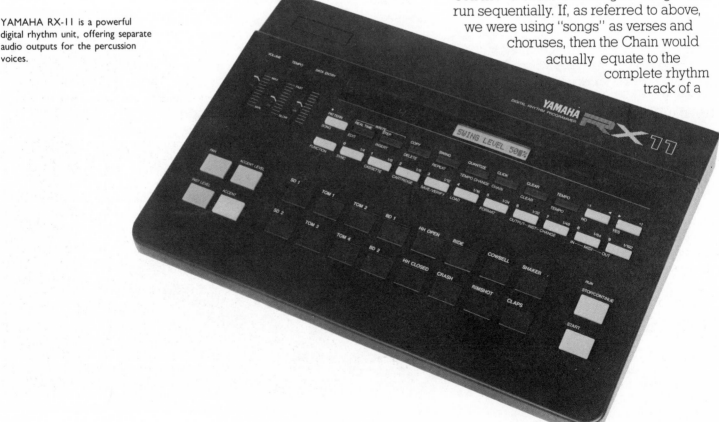

piece, which might therefore look something like this:

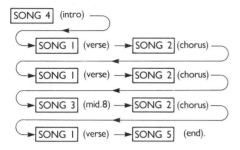

If, however, each "song" had been recorded as a song (i.e. a complete rhythmic track to a piece) then the Chain facility could be used to run complete songs concurrently - thus you could program the rhythm machine to provide the drum track for a series of separate numbers - *Fig. 4.01* illustrates this with reference to an LP record.

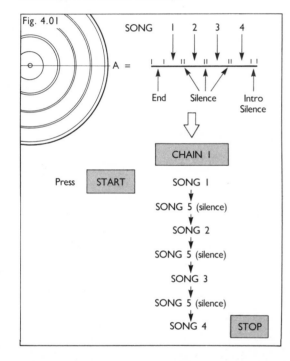

Rhythm Patterns

For the moment let us consider a rhythm pattern to consist of a single bar of music, with the pattern in common time - 4 beats to the bar.

The whole concept behind the rhythm unit is that patterns are divided into a certain number of equal steps, and that you can set the triggering of a particular drum sound at any of these step points. So if we were to have a bar of music relating to a snare drum that appeared thus:

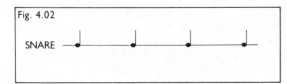

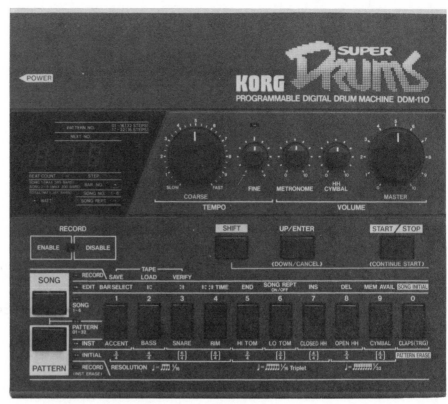

KORG DDM-110. The first low cost drum machine utilising voices that have been recorded digitally.

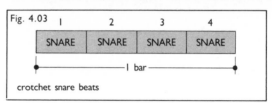

Fig. 4.03

	1	2	3	4
	SNARE	SNARE	SNARE	SNARE

— 1 bar —

crotchet snare beats

we would need to be able to split the bar up into four equal steps and to set a trigger point at each step. So by dividing the pattern into four steps we can handle crotchets (quarter notes) - shown diagrammatically in *Fig. 4.03*. But should

KORG DDM-220. The first rhythm unit to produce purely percussion (as opposed to drum), voices, using digital technology.

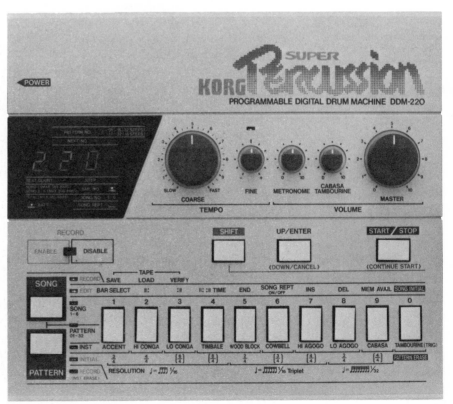

you wish to be able to program quavers then the resolution of having a bar divided by four is not enough - the bar would have to be divided into 8 steps.

Take for example the simple pattern shown in *Fig. 4.04*. Here we have four percussion voices - bass, snare, tom, and cymbal. The shortest note is a semi-quaver (a sixteenth note), so the bar has to be divided into 16 steps in order to accommodate this size of note. The diagrammatic representation of this rhythm showing on which beats the various percussion voices fall is known as matrix notation.

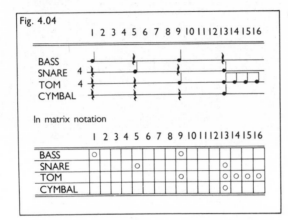

It would obviously seem better to divide the bar into as many steps as possible so that as wide a range of note values as possible can be utilised. If you listen to a live drummer, you will notice that he will play notes that don't fall exactly on the beat, and in this way he gives his drumming 'feel'. By dividing the pattern into say 256, you could specify the position of a note to 1/256th (a quarter of a sixty-

fourth note) facilitating the programming of patterns which took into account this element of human 'feel'. But unfortunately the greater the resolution the more memory the rhythm unit requires and consequently the more expensive it becomes.

Typical low-cost rhythm units utilise a 16-step resolution, whilst the more expensive units will facilitate bar division from 1/192 to 1/1536. Why such strange numbers? Well, not all rhythm patterns are in 4/4 time, and even those that are will often incorporate triplets (three notes that occupy the space of two). So with a pattern in which the resolution is set to 1/64, a 192 step bar would accommodate sixty-fourth-note triplets.

The 1536 division bar is used only by the most advanced rhythm units, and is particularly suited for machines that are programmed in real time (see later). The low-cost rhythm units offer 12-step patterns to accommodate 3/4 patterns, thus enabling sixteenth notes to be programmed in.

So far we have considered the single bar pattern, but some rhythm machines offer the option of two (or more) bar patterns. Even some low cost units provide this facility, and of course instead of programming two-bar patterns you could double the resolution of the pattern by using two bars as one. For example, if we had two 16-step bars we could play the bars back in performance mode at double speed, and so have a 32-step pattern.

Fig. 4.05 shows a pattern that could be programmed on a mid-priced drum machine. Here we have 32-step resolution and eight different instrument voices. The

Fig. 4.05

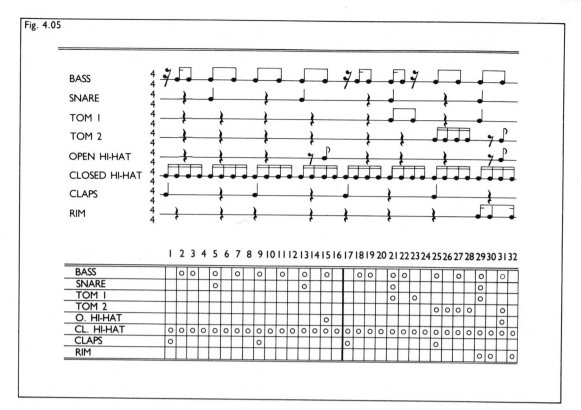

actual mechanics of programming the pattern will be dealt with later in this chapter, but in Appendix A you will find a range of standard rhythm patterns shown in both musical and matrix notation. These include certain patterns that you will tend to find in pre-programmed rhythm machines.

Tempo, Clocks and Counters

Having pressed the START, or PLAY, button on a rhythm machine it is the clock that determines the rate at which the pattern is stepped through. The clock is simply a device that puts out regular pulses, and for every pulse the pattern advances one step. It follows therefore that a 64-step pattern requires 64 clock pulses to occur for the complete pattern to be played.

The rate at which the clock runs is known as the Tempo and in keeping with traditional notation it is measured in beats per minute. This doesn't directly correspond to the number of clock beats per minute.

Consider the two following examples (see *Fig. 4.06*):

1) Tempo = 120 beats per minute, and there are 16 steps per bar.

therefore each beat requires
$$16/4 = 4 \text{ clock pulses}$$
so clock rate $= 120 \times 4$
$= 480$ pulses per min.

2) Tempo = 120 beats per minute, and there are 64 steps per bar

therefore each beat requires
$$64/4 = 16 \text{ clock pulses}$$
so clock rate $= 120 \times 16$
$= 1920$ pulses per min.

So you can see that an increased resolution requires a faster clock pulse.

Digital Handling

This section is not of major importance in the understanding of rhythm units as it

Fig. 4.06

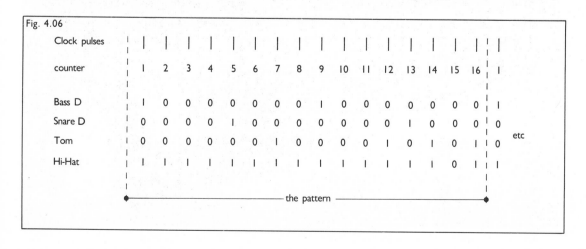

concerns the way in which the actual digital control circuitry and memory works. Nevertheless it may be of help in trying to grasp the fundamentals involved.

The beauty of a 'simple' drum machine is that at any step either a drum beat occurs or it doesn't, i.e. it's ON or OFF. This bi-state situation lends itself beautifully to digital control circuit techniques.

Now say, as shown earlier, we have a simple 4×16 matrix pattern. That is to say 8 percussion voices utilised within a 16 step pattern. We can store this pattern in a 4×16 memory circuit as shown in *Fig. 4.06* You will notice that there are four outputs, corresponding to the four triggers that are sent to the percussion voices, and an address input. (For simplicity's sake we'll consider the workings of this device's clock in decimal numbers rather than in binary which is the number base to which digital circuits actually function.)

When the start button is pressed for the rhythm unit to play back its pattern the first clock pulse is sent to counter. This in turn causes the number "1" (in digital code) to appear at its output. This number is sent to the address input of the memory circuit, and causes the contents of step one of the memory to appear at the four corresponding outputs. If a voice were to sound at that step, the output would go from zero to maximum, and this information would be sent to that particular percussion voice, causing it to sound.

If the voice isn't to be triggered then the output will remain zero.

The next clock pulse causes the counter to advance to "2" and the settings corresponding to step 2 are now to be found at the four outputs. And so the process continues until step 16 is reached,

after which the counter reverts to "1" and the pattern is played over again. Naturally, by altering the clock rate, the speed at which the pattern is played varies in direct proportion.

Real Time and Step Time Programming

Having looked at the way in which patterns are stored in the controller's memory, we should now examine the two main ways in which patterns are programmed into a rhythm unit.

There are two distinct methods, step time and real time programming. Step time programming involves the filling in of the pattern matrix bit by bit. A typical programming sequence of events might run as follows:

★ Select a particular voice (say bass drum).
★ Step through the 16 (say) steps using YES and NO buttons. If you want the drum to sound at that particular step press "YES", if not "NO".
★ At the end of the pattern select a new percussion voice and repeat the procedure.
★ Go into performance mode and listen to your pattern to see if it is as desired.

Programming in step time is as simple as that. Some rhythm units feature a Liquid Crystal Display that depicts the pattern matrix so you can get a visual representation of the pattern. This makes editing of individual notes far easier.

Real Time programming involves a somewhat different procedure. It is in fact rather like making a

Fig. 4.07
Yamaha RX-21, a low cost drum machine utilising digital voices. The buttons can be played in real time either on their own or along with the programme pattern.

recording using a tape recorder.
Fig. 4.07 shows a rhythm unit with which you can program real time patterns. You will notice that on the front panel there is a set of buttons that correspond to the individual voices of the machine. To program a pattern using a more elaborate unit you first need to specify how many bars the pattern is going to require, and the time signature. The instrument is then switched into record mode and you will hear a metronome pulse. Say we were recording a two-bar common time pattern, then the metronome would probably count out the quarter notes, with an emphasis on the first beat of each bar. The pattern can then be played using the buttons.

There are various techniques which can be employed here to get the best results. Some people prefer to start with the bass drum and put down just that first. When the end of the second bar is reached, the pattern resets and plays itself back over, with the recorded bass drum. You can then move to, say, the snare and overdub that. And so on.

A few drum machine users like to try to play the pattern straight off. This is tricky, and only drummers with experience of conventional kits can usually get away with this kind of programming.

Having programmed your pattern into the drum machine you can revert to performance mode and recall the pattern as and when necessary.

Quantization

Although it might seem that real time programming is a much better system as it allows you to program "feel" into the pattern, this isn't necessarily the case. A drum machine that facilitates real time programming still functions as described above. The pattern is still divided up into so many discrete steps, and each note has to be set on a step. If you record a pattern with notes that don't fall on the step points then they are automatically corrected so that they do. This is known as Quantization (see *Fig. 4.08*) and it sets the minimum time interval between the notes of the pattern.

Quantization isn't necessarily a bad thing as it can be turned round and used to the programmer's advantage. For

ROLAND TR-909
A MIDI version of Roland's successful TR-808, equipped with digital voices.

example, if you weren't particularly accurate in playing the pattern, the controller's circuitry will pull the pattern "in" to the nearest beat - i.e. it can clear up any shortcomings in the timing skills of the player. The converse of this is also true in that if you are a good player, and want to inject extra 'feel' into the pattern you may be thwarted by the quantization effect. It obviously depends on the severity of the quantization.

Many machines offer a variable degree of quantization. You might want to set the quantization to 1/16 when recording the bass drum and snare - in which case these voices would be pulled in to the nearest sixteenth note (semi-quaver). The quantization could then be set to, say, 1/64 enabling much shorter notes to be recorded, then maybe turned off (which equates to a very high setting as 1/192) for, say, a roll round the toms. So quantization has its uses.

Swing

One criticism often made of the rhythm unit (half prompted by the nomenclature of drum machine), is its unerring adherence to the beat. Manufacturers have sought several different ways to introduce a "real-feel" to the sound. One of which is often termed "Swing".

Imagine that a rhythm pattern is divided up into 16 steps, and we were considering a straight hi-hat beat on every semi-quaver (sixteenth note) as depicted in *Fig. 4.09a*. The introduction of the Swing effect would seek to move every other note a fraction before, or after, the beat. Just a small

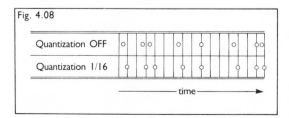

Fig. 4.08

Quantization OFF										
Quantization 1/16										

———— time ————→

variation here can inject considerable life into the patten, though the effect is somewhat more useful in a jazz orientated context.

The Swing effect is measured as a percentage, with a 50% value having no effect. Usually a percentage of less than 50% moves the note before the beat, and a higher one behind the beat, though this does vary from machine to machine. *Fig. 4.09b.*

Fig. 4.09a/b	
a) SWING OFF	o o o o o o o o o o o o o o o o
b) SWING ON	oo oo oo oo oo oo oo oo oo

———————— time ————————➤

Specific Voicing Information

So far we've considered only the programming of notes - i.e. when each note should fall within the pattern. But, as any acoustic drummer will confirm, there are many other important parameters to consider in order to give the rhythm pattern an authentic feel. Every time you hit the skin of a drum you do so in a slightly different way - you may strike the playing surface with a different force, or you may hit the skin at a different position - either way the actual quality of the sound will be different.

As mentioned in Chapter 1 there are three elemental fundamental principles that define any sounds we hear: Pitch, Timbre, and Loudness. The way in which the drum is struck affects all three of these in one way or another. When utilising a drum machine you usually have control over just the volume of each note, although in some instances timbre and pitch can be varied.

Programming of Loudness and Accents

There are various degrees to which drum machines allow the programming of the loudness of each note. Let's start with the simplest function - Accents.

An accented note is one which is set to sound louder than normal.

There are three grades of Accent, dependent on the sophistication of the drum machine you are using:

1) non-related polyphonic accenting: a good drum machine will allow you to accent any note of the pattern. In this case each percussive voice will have a normal and an accented level. So, for example, each normal snare note will sound at a

particular level, and all accented snare notes will sound at a different (greater) level. The increase in amplitude between accented and non-accented notes will vary from voice to voice.

2) related polyphonic accenting: in this instance the difference between accented and non-accented notes is the same for all voices.

3) monophonic accenting: with some budget drum machines, you have to accent all notes for a particular step if you wish to use this facility. See *Fig. 4.10*.

Fig. 4.10	1	2	3	4	5	6	7	8	9	10	11	12	13	14	15	16
Bass D	o								o							
Snare D					o								o			
Tom								o				o		o		o
Hi-Hat	o	o	o	o	o	o	o	o	o	o	o	o	o	o		o
ACCENT	o								o				o			

In this latter case the Accent facility is programmed as part of the pattern matrix as if it were another voice.

Some units offer a Mute facility. This behaves in a similar fashion to the Accent, only when activated the level of that voice is reduced from a normal value to the muted one. So if the rhythm composer offers this mute facility each voice can be triggered at three levels: Muted, Normal, and Accented.

More sophisticated units that enable you to give each drum note a specific amplitude are available. Two methods are used to enter the information:

1) Each beat has to be entered separately, the level at which that beat is to be recorded must be entered before the note, or series of notes (if they are all to be at the same level) is played. This is slow.

2) Some form of external controller is used, e.g. a velocity sensitive keyboard or some drum pads. The notes are then played on the controller with dynamics, and the information fed to the rhythm unit (normally utilising the MIDI link). This is much better, though it does rely on the need for some form of external control device.

Fully variable programming of accents is very important if you want to get the most out of your rhythm unit in terms of expression. Also, the use of this facility is really the only way to effectively program a realistic sounding drum roll into a pattern. And even then if every note sounds exactly the same the roll will still sound artificial.

Programmable Voice Pitching

Some instruments that use digital voices offer the facility to record a specific tuning for each beat. This is a similar feature to programmable accents (see *Fig. 4.12*) but in this case a pitch can be assigned to each note as opposed to (or as well as) an amplitude. This facility vastly enhances the range of the voice complement of an instrument. For example if the tuning of a Tom can be varied over a two octave range in semitone steps, it's almost like having a 24 Tom kit. This isn't strictly true as shown in *Fig. 4.11a*. As you can see, if we were playing two Tom notes at different pitches in close succession to one another utilising just one voice, then the decay of one would be interrupted by the new note. This would not sound right. So to effectively and realistically achieve the desired effect at least two separate Tom voices are necessary - *Fig. 4.11b*.

Being able to tune a particular voice is useful in achieving greater realism. A snare hit hard will sound somewhat sharper in pitch than one hit more gently. This can be accommodated in the programming.

Another advantage of programmable voice pitching lies in being able to vastly alter the nature of a sound. For example, a crash cymbal played at a pitch a couple of octaves down sounds very like a large gong, and a floor tom can be translated, by raising its pitch, into a roto-tom etc.

Outputs

A drum machine will offer one (sometimes more) of four kinds of audio line outputs:

1) *Mono Output*: A single output jack which gives a mix of all the voices is provided. This output is used when driving into a single channel amplifier and is usually the only kind of output found on the less expensive units.

2) *Stereo Output (fixed panning)*. Here the outputs of the instruments have been arranged so that they are positioned across the stereo image. You will have left and right output sockets, one of which may be labelled MIX, or MONO (for use with a single channel amp).

3) *Stereo Output (variable panning)*. As above but with the ability to position each individual voice anywhere across the stereo image. Being able to pan the instruments is very useful, since as well

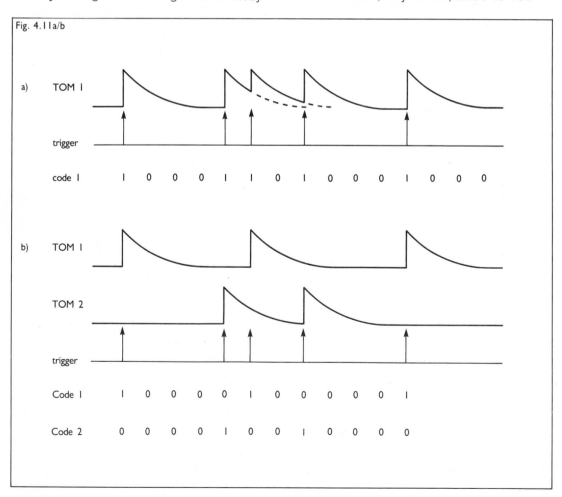

Fig. 4.11a/b

as being able to create your own stereo kit, you can also isolate a particular voice for individual treatment by panning it to the left (say), and all the other voices to the right. The snare can now be separately processed with parametric EQ, gated reverb, echo, or whatever.

4) *Separate Outputs*. Having a separate output for each voice is essential for a professional rhythm unit as it allows individual treatment of each percussive voice. You will need a separate mixer in order to effectively utilise this facility. See *Fig. 4.12*.

Drum Machines: A Brief History

A drum machine is simply an automatic device that plays the drums. It could therefore be argued that automatic drummers have been around since the fairground organs of the 19th century. These steam powered machines had real drums and cymbals mounted inside the calliope itself and were actually played with pneumatically driven sticks. The latest generation of drum machines doesn't have to be horse drawn, nor do they need a plentiful supply of clean water, but like fairground organs they do reflect the technology of the time.

The mighty Wurlitzer organ which used to appear majestically from the pit of all the best cinemas also had its own integrated drummer. At least half a century separates the Wurlitzer from the preset rhythm boxes of the Seventies, but their functions are almost identical.

It was the organ companies that did the most to promote the use of the automatic drummer. The home organ became the mid-20th century's alternative to the pianoforte, and the manufacturing companies strove to provide their instruments with as many facilities as possible, enabling their customers to emulate a complete band.

It soon became clear that there was a market for self contained drum boxes, and the organ companies were well poised to fill the gap. The Bentley Rhythm Ace was one of the most successful preset rhythm units of latter years, and in fact it was used by contemporary figures of the Sixties and Seventies such as Arthur Brown and Elton John.

During the mid part of this century a set of completely different dance rhythms had evolved, but this didn't stop Japanese companies such as Korg or Roland from marketing such patterns as Foxtrot, Samba, and of course the 'well-known' Enka on their original drummer replacement

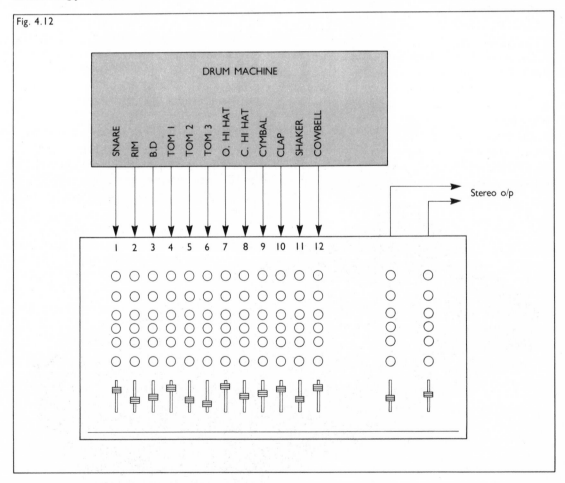

Fig. 4.12

products. These boxes were again designed to sit on top of the traditionally styled pianos and organs and so were designed to match the mahogany veneered cases. The very first product of the aforementioned Korg company, who now make respected synthesizers and signal processing equipment, was in fact a drum machine.

Many systems evolved for the automatic production of rhythm patterns. Streetly electronics, the people responsible for the Mellotron, even used an eight-track cartridge player - to change a rhythm one simply replaced the cartridge. Unfortunately the sounds weren't of a particularly high fidelity, and the necessary tape rewinding was slow, thus causing the product to enjoy very limited success.

All the machines mentioned so far used analogue circuitry for the voices. It wasn't until Roger Linn came along that digitally encapsulated sounds were used. Roger Linn was a recording engineer who realised that if you put a drum beat into a digital delay line unit you could retrieve it any time you wanted. So the replacement or rechannelling of the studio drummer began in earnest. Bands, musicians and producers could actually go into the recording studio with a drum track already planned and executed. The drummer could then over-dub real drums at a much later stage to strengthen the arrangement. This was not exactly a "Rock 'n Roll" way of making scintillating music, but popular recordings of the period were, at that time, veering away from spontaneity anyway.

Linn subsequently moved to the 9000 which was a considerably more sophisticated touch sensitive machine with full dynamics and having the added advantage of being an editable 32-track keyboard recorder.

The digital drum machine subsequently became increasingly affordable,

ROLAND TR-707. Note the liquid crystal display, which maps out the pattern you are programming. To the left of this display is a cartridge slot enabling the user to plug in memory cartridges upon which can be stored rhythm patterns.

and as a result more popular. Not only could you purchase a drum machine with drum sounds, but kits specially designed to produce Latin instruments soon evolved.

Sequential Inc (formerly Sequential Circuits Inc) have been up with the front-runners in the new development stakes. Their Drumtraks was the first to offer programmable voice tuning and programmable voice levels. And their Tom model featured separate plug-in cartridges containing different sets of voices (e.g. Latins, Electronics, etc.).

From using pre-recorded digital voices, the obvious step was to enable the musician or producer to load his own sounds into the instrument. E-MU Systems were one of the first companies to offer such a facility with their SP-12 Drum Computer. And in 1986 Casio brought the realm of sampling drum machines within the reach of most people's pockets with their RZ-1 unit which can be quickly loaded with up to four different percussion voices.

The evolution of Sampling Drum machines marks the most recent quantum jump in this field. As to what the next one will be, time alone will tell.

The Sequential Drumtraks. The first drum machine enabling the user to program loudness and pitch for every single note. With the Drumtraks you can set each voice to any one of 16 different pitches, or amplitudes, thus you can access 16 different Toms, say, within a single pattern.

CHAPTER 5
ELECTRONIC KIT

Introduction

The electronic drum kit (EDK) demonstrates what technology can offer the conventional acoustic drummer. The EDK utilises a set of electronic voice modules to create percussive sounds. These are controlled by a set of pads that are played in a similar fashion to conventional drums - i.e. they are hit (albeit with sticks or just hands). The EDK, unlike the rhythm unit, is primarily a real time instrument. It sounds as you hit it.

The EDK has really become accepted only since the early 1980s, but since its inception, primarily due to the pioneering work of UK based company Simmons Electronics, the EDK is a commonly accepted feature of most of today's contemporary bands.

The advantages of the EDK over the acoustic kit are numerous. It offers an infinite variety of sounds, it is dynamic, compact,

easy to amplify, etc. But it would seem unlikely that the electronic kit could ever completely replace its acoustic counterpart, primarily because no matter how good the sounds and feel of the kit become, it will always require amplification of some sort. EDKs and acoustic kits sit happily beside one another, and the two easily lend themselves to combinational set-ups, thus giving the drummer the best of both worlds. *Fig. 5.01*

The EDK consists of two main elements: the electronic voices that produce the sounds (normally housed in a single box known as the brain), and the control pads which dictate when and how that sound occurs *(Fig. 5.02)*.

We have already looked at percussion voices, so the majority of this chapter will be devoted to the subject of the controllers, or playing pads.

Fig. 5.01

SIMMONS pads with acoustic cymbals mounted on specially developed tubular frame.

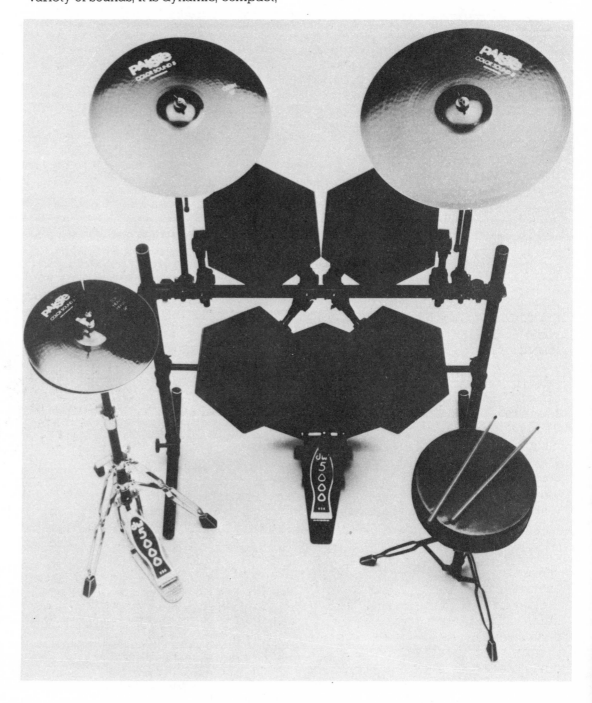

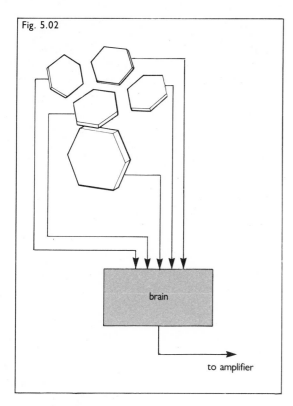

Fig. 5.02

to amplifier

The pads when hit send a dynamic trigger pulse to the ''brain'' which houses the voices which generate the sound. When triggered, a specific percussive sound is generated, which can then be amplified.

The Pads

When we strike an acoustic drum, what is happening? There are two prime parameters that affect the response of that drum:

1) How hard the drum was hit.
2) Where on its playing surface it was hit.

These two functions determine the volume and the timbre of the sound emanating from that particular drum. The EDK's pad set therefore has to be able to pass at least the first, and ideally both, these bits of information to the percussion voice modules in order for the EDK to have an authentic and useful response.

All electronic drum pads have something inside them called a transducer which senses the vibrations produced by the stick striking them. These vibrations are then carried to the 'brain' in the form of micro-currents which, once they arrive, stimulate the 'brain's' oscillators. The most commonly found variety of such transducers are known as piezos (piezo electric transducers). A transducer is simply a very small loudspeaker working like a microphone; it senses a vibration and creates a voltage equivalent. These pick-ups are about the size of a ten pence piece and either stuck directly to the bottom of the playing surface, or set in foam just below it. The optimum position for the transducer seems to be just off-centre, this position saves it from being wrecked by direct hits from the stick. Since they came

into being, electronic drum pads have had several different kinds of playing surface. Simmons SDS 3 and Syndrum both used 'real', plastic drum heads, which were of course, tuneable, while Synare had tin lids with 'ping pong' bat type rubber. The Simmons SDS 5, the pad which started it all, was made from 'riot shield' type plastic. However, just recently there's been a move back to real drum heads.

In the main, the pads are formed like plastic bowls with close fitting lids on, rather like storage containers. (As a matter of fact, some bright sparks in the very late 70s actually did produce an instrument called Humdrum which really did use Tupperware to hold its electronics!).

Pads are generally packed inside with foam rubber to give them a less oppressive natural sound and to protect the transducer. Simmons have always surrounded the stress points within the pad (where the wires join to transducer and output socket), with rubbery, non-setting gel. But, several other manufacturers did not take this precaution, and ultimately paid the price when their units broke down.

Frequently, to give the pad a little more weight, a piece of shaped plywood will be fixed inside it, this will form a playing surface too, once covered with a suitable material e.g. rubber. See *Fig. 5.03*

Fig. 5.03
The construction of a Simmons electronic drum pad. The pickup(s) is mounted on an internal plastic moulding upon which sits the rubber playing surface. The entire workings are housed in a high impact vacuum formed enclosure with the traditional six-sided Simmons design.

As stated, ideally it is necessary to know not only how hard the pad is hit, but also where. Simmons developed a system (used in their SDS 9 kit) whereby a pair of identical transducers are mounted inside the pad See *Fig. 5.04*. The second one is set much closer to the edge to pick up the vibrations there. And from the information derived from both transducers the brain can determine exactly where on the pad the stick struck, and produce a corresponding timbre.

Fig. 5.04

Two transducers are used, one in the centre, one on the rim. From this the 'brain' can calculate where exactly the pad is hit.

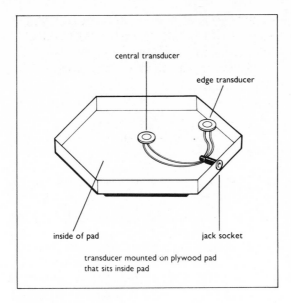

transducer mounted on plywood pad that sits inside pad

Support System

Most manufacturers favour conventional hardware for their pads, based on the tripod stands used by acoustic drum sets to support cymbals, or tom toms, see *Fig. 5.05*.

An alternative but more expensive method to mount EDKs originates from America. Instead of two tripod based stands, this support system has four legs which are joined horizontally by three cross pieces. This makes for a very stable

framework and the actual Tom arms from the original set fit comfortably into holders which are built into it. The frame is designed to support the bass drum pad too, and it accomplishes this much more successfully than the spurs supplied by any other manufacturer. (All free standing bass drum pads have an annoying tendency to move away from the player when they're hit. (see *Fig. 5.01*)

Playing Techniques
Snare and Toms

Most modern electronic drum kits with their more resilient pads can be played with more or less the same techniques as 'genuine' drums (i.e. drums formed by a membrane being stretched across a hollow tube). However, some of the original pads and a few of the latest ones have a very hard playing surface which necessitates a different, more economical approach. Drummers coming from acoustic kits to the hard plastic playing surfaces of some EDKs would tend to hit with unnecessary force, causing complications.

The early pads had something of a 'table-top' feel about them, and whilst it was possible to hit them hard for a short period of time without mishap, many busy

Fig. 5.05

SIMMONS SDS-800
The SDS-8 features bass drum, snare drum and two toms which are connected to a brain (not shown).

studio players might find themselves playing them for hours on end. Then they would really know they'd been in a battle. It would invariably be the elbows which began to suffer from the constant jarring. This pain had an effect on the player, and forced him to 'lighten-up' in his approach to EDKs.

This side-effect of the playing-pad had a more fundamental and positive effect on at least one manufacturer. Simmons Electronics resolved to produce a pad which would not injure the player, and which would feel very like a real drum. Even though the original generation of EDKs had sensitivity controls that enabled the player to adjust the response of each pad, they were invariably 'over sensitive' and important nuances like grace notes would be impossible to accomplish. This was because even a soft hit invariably came out relatively loud, so a 'flam', (a loud beat preceded by a softer one), would not sound the same. Neither would a 'ruff' nor many more of the 26 rudiments.

Any unintentional (or intentional) resting of the stick on the pad would give rise to what can only be described as a motorbike revving noise, so a good technique which lifts the stick away from the pad immediately after the stroke will give the best results. (Rather in the style of a military drummer). It should be noted though that all these idiosyncracies are not prevalent in modern EDKs. Up-to-date pads are designed to play exactly like acoustic drums.

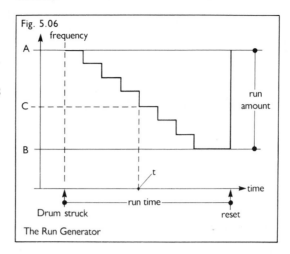

Fig. 5.06

The Run Generator

The Run Generator

A 'run generator' is a facility designed to enhance the voice production of a kit. It forms part of the brain's electronics, and isn't strictly part of the controller mechanism. This feature allows a single Tom voice to sound like several, i.e. by constantly hitting the same pad, you can arrange for the pitch of the voice to vary with each note. See *Fig. 5.06*.

THE RUN GENERATOR
Two parameters need to be set, the Run Time and the Run Amount. If the voice is set to pitch "A", then the Run Amount control will determine the deviation from this pitch, in this case to Pitch "B". The Run Time control determines how long the pitch takes to fall from A to B.

When the drum is struck the cycle begins, and the pitch steps down eventually reaching pitch B, whence it resets to "A". If the drum is hit at any point in the cycle, its pitch will correspond to the current step in the ladder, so after time T, the pitch would be "C".

SIMMONS pads on tubular frame. The frame enables the drummer to position the pads exactly how he wants and also provides an extremely strong and stable support.

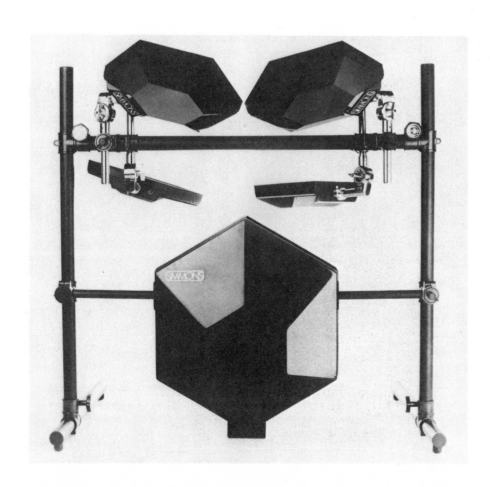

Some companies utilise run generators, that can be interrupted, usually via a foot pedal, so the pitch can be held at the designated value until the pedal is released. Another pedal will return the generator to the top of its cycle. Both systems are able to move down, or up, through the tom sounds, and are definitely an asset to an electronic set.

Other Effects

Repeat, echo and 'slap back' are available on certain EDKs, and these features need to be experimented with. The 'slap back' is simply an Elvis Presley style single repeat which is adjustable; the repeat though is much more like a digital delay. By increasing the number of repeats you can produce echo effects. See *Fig. 5.07*.

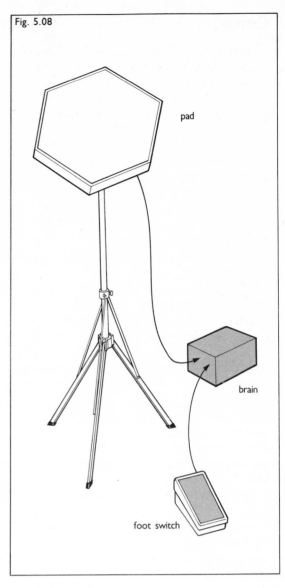

Fig. 5.08

pad

brain

foot switch

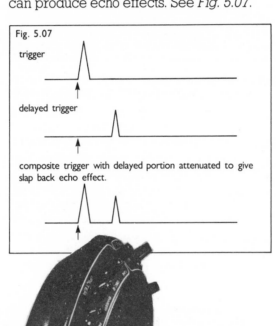

Fig. 5.07

trigger

delayed trigger

composite trigger with delayed portion attenuated to give slap back echo effect.

SYNARE BD-2 BASS DRUM STAND
The early-day solution to having a synthesized bass drum.

Bass Drum Pad

To all intents and purposes the bass drum pad is played just the same as an ordinary drum. Of course there's not quite so much bounce from those examples which have 'piston-loaded' centres, but here too practice makes perfect.

Hi-Hat

To a limited extent hi-hat pedals are available too. These are joined to a pad and serve to simulate the opening and closing of the cymbals. See *Fig. 5.08*. These cymbals are digitally sampled and the foot pedal allows you to have the variables of closed, open and half open hi-hat sounds. You can also have the more subtle 'click' sound, achieved when the two cymbals click together. Simply press and release the foot pedal.

Cymbals

Cymbals are available too for EDKs, but so far no company has come up with a really convincing example. The problem has been that to capture the complicated tones and overtones of a really good instrument requires a great deal of expensive memory. So far this is not available at a realistic price, but the state of the art being what it is, we shouldn't have to wait too long.

Recording Techniques

There are of course many different ways of recording an electronic drum set, but if you're 'putting down' as part of a 'bed track', then the first thing to do is to get the speaker foldback to the drummer in the studio before he begins to work on his sound. Speakers are preferable because headphones, which are more convenient, fit tightly to the head and use the cranium as a speaker cabinet, and are deceptive in their bottom end response. You find out later that the drums are lacking in bass. Once you've set up your sounds the simplest method of getting them to tape is via direct injection. Simply join from the back of the 'brain' straight to the mixing desk, one channel for each drum. The stereo output is not frequently used (unless you're short of tracks), because the 'picture' it produces is often fixed, and not very subtle. It consists of hard right, hard left and dead centre. Often, the cabinet which was used to get the drummers sound originally, will be miked up and recorded on its own track to widen the sound (an ambient alternative to digital reverberation).

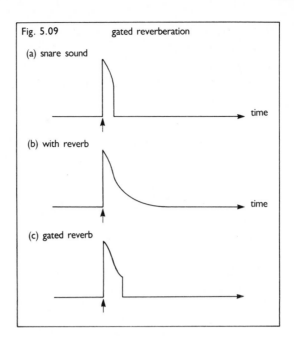

Fig. 5.09   gated reverberation

(a) snare sound

time

(b) with reverb

time

(c) gated reverb

Many experienced session players will have their very own 'pet' sounds within the memory of their EDK, and will be able to dial them up as necessary. These sounds will have been worked on elsewhere, but often the producer will want to have a totally different new sound. Once you start to get decent sounds from the 'brain', equalisation and effects are added from the mixing desk.

For the most part, the snare drum would need some form of reverb to give it space. The AMS reverb is a favourite because it works well on percussive sounds and contributes to the overall aggression. Gated plate or gated room reverb (see *Fig. 5.09*) doesn't really work so well on synthesized drums because the white noise within their sound tends to appear distorted when you restrict (i.e. gate) the length of a long reverb. It does, though, work

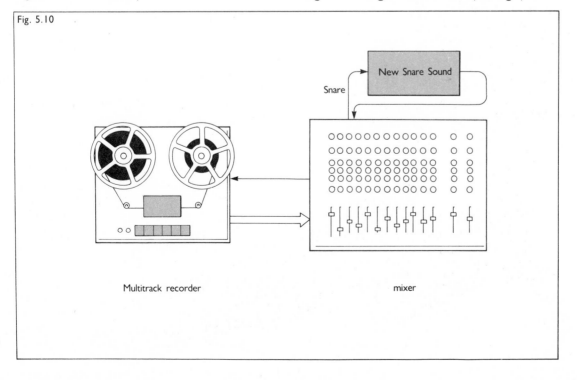

Fig. 5.10

New Snare Sound

Snare

Multitrack recorder   mixer

very well on acoustic snare drums. Tom toms tend to benefit from reverb too, but flanging is a very viable alternative, especially when the toms are playing on their own. Delay is also usable (i.e. Slapback) but of course the only way to know is to try the alternatives. (Our old friend the room speaker works well on toms too but isn't really used for bass or snare drums.)

A very good effect for the bass drum is a simple low cost digital reverb which can create an illusion of space without increasing the drum's click.

Triggering and Time Shifting

It is possible to trigger an EDK 'brain' from tape but it can be tricky. This is something you'd want to do if you weren't satisfied with the sound you already had on tape. see *Fig. 5.10*. Obviously the drums you wish to re-trigger must be on their own tracks, so bass and snare are the obvious candidates. The problem is that invariably a delay of roughly 5 milliseconds will occur. This can be very off-putting and is more obvious with a fast track where it tends to give the impression that the drummer is playing out of time. As illustrated in *Fig. 5.11*

a) The drum falls behind the bar lines
b) The sound is compressed and gated
c) The tape is reversed so that the drum falls before the beat
d) The drum is then delayed so that it falls on the beat
e) When the tape is then reversed the drum sounds perfectly on the beat.

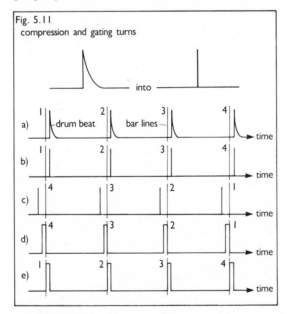

Fig. 5.11
compression and gating turns

it is possible to get rid of this 'false triggering' by using a compressor, first to squash the signal from the tape, then 'gating' it to get a fast attack time with little or no decay. Then we must turn the tape over so that the last track becomes the first, and delay the signal through any good quality digital unit. This delayed signal must now be recorded onto a spare track and when the tape is then turned over and played the right way you will have a pulse slightly in advance of the beat in question. It's child's play to utilise the

same digital delay to adjust the position of the pulse (in real time) and then trigger the synthesized drum voice. Several units are available to achieve exactly the same correction of signal from tape, but they do veer towards the expensive, and do not tend to be used all that often.

Electronic drums may also be used for overdubs, when they tend to be set up in the control room itself. The purpose of this sort of overdubbing is obviously to replace drums which were originally there, be they acoustic or synthesized. The older EDKs needed to be monitored very loudly because of the acoustic sound of the stick hitting the pad. It really was most off-putting and engineers were often forced to wear headphones to concentrate. The newer ones have a much lower click, and are much less obtrusive. Normally one would plug the 'brain' straight into the mixing desk, set the inherent sounds and then use all the same effects we've already discussed.

Sampling and Freezing

There is another way of 'creating' drum sounds in the studio which is to do with the most sophisticated of the digital delay units. More expensive delays will freeze any sound you desire using digital conversion and retain them in their memory. So, every time you wish to extract it, you simply need to trigger the delay manually or automatically. It's not difficult, though not particularly honest. To sample from tape or disc just locate the sound you want and insert it into the delay (you can subsequently edit out unwanted parts).

Amplification

A consideration often overlooked in the euphoria of buying an EDK is that ultimately you are going to have to acquire something to amplify it. This, it must be said, is not going to be cheap if you want to do it well. With an amplification system you most definitely get what you pay for.

The one piece of amplification equipment which will not work effectively with electronic drums is that old workhorse the lead guitar combo. For those of you not in the know, a Combo has its amplifier and speaker(s) in the same box, often with an open back. One of these is not really sufficient to cope with the 'bottom end' produced by an EDK. What you ideally need to combine in a system for this purpose is a very powerful bass rig for this 'bottom end', an undistorted guitar-type amp. for the 'middle' attack, and finally, some sort of horns or tweeters to give clarity and sibilance to the high end. You also need an amplifier with a large dynamic range, a wide frequency spectrum, and large peaks of short-term power. So far the 'up-market' keyboard player's rig will almost fulfil those requirements, and he or she is likely to have a mixer and effects rack to further shape the sound and make it more interesting (*almost*, only, because by and large a keyboard player's rig does not have to cope with the dynamics at the bottom end resulting from the bass drum's constant battering. Specifically, a bass drum needs a couple of hundred watts to be audible, and even then may be working flat out and distort).

Simmons, however, are the only company to introduce their own amplifier designed especially for EDKs. This is in fact a combo, but a very special one. See *Fig. 5.12*

A mixer will allow much greater control over all the voices because you'll set it up so that each voice (snare, bass, toms etc.) will have its own channel and its own equalisation control. Thus you will be able to add 'top' to the snare drum without the bass drum beginning to click. This will also allow you to use the 'mix' output from the drum brain, and save channels in the P.A. mixer.

To recap, by and large only a P.A. rig will provide all the facilities that an electronic set needs, and even a scaled down version of a 'front of house' system will be expensive.

The best bet is to put your set immediately into the main P.A. and then get some way to 'monitor' yourself. Hopefully the P.A. will consist of several different sized boxes rather than one with speaker columns. (Columns can work for drums, but only if they've got closed backs and several are bolted together.)

A keyboard amplifier (rather like a guitar Combo but with better full frequency capability) will work as a monitor, but not as a main amp. ('Cube' amplifiers will also function with reasonable efficiency in this capacity; especially if you use several.)

One of the larger German amplifier companies (who also make digitally sampled EDKs) has a bass amp. with a seven band 'graphic' which will pretty well reproduce all of the necessary tone colours. Conveniently it has a 'Direct' output (to the P.A.) and a 'send and return' to allow you to put echo or what have you over the whole kit. If used with a small mixer it could prove satisfactory.

If you find this whole amplifier acquisition daunting, don't despair. The biggest growth area in the amplifier world is that of electronic percussion reproduction. And many new developments are on the horizon. However, one thing should be borne in mind, amplifying demanding instruments such as EDKs will never be cheap.

EDKs - A Brief History

The first modern synthesized drum set was invented more or less by accident in, believe it or not, 1963. An American called Stephen Lamme was working on a practice set for his son; he wanted it to be soundless to his neighbours yet audible and stimulating to his offspring.

For a while, his son was content to be stimulated through headphones but one day he wondered just how his practice set would sound through an amplifier. That was it, the synthesized, amplified, solid-bodied drum set had arrived. Ultimately the sets were refined and marketed under the name "Impakt", but in truth they didn't really live up to their name and failed to capture the world's imagination.

However, there was a drum that did. It was never a set, simply an add-on for an acoustic drum kit, and called Syndrum. Its inventor was a one-time Beach Boys drummer named Joe Pollard who was working on his brainchild in the late Sixties. Anyone familiar with the music of the Seventies will remember the sound of the Syndrum; it was high-pitched, obtrusive, and absolutely "done-to-death". No hit record or TV commercial was complete without it; and this over use ultimately contributed to the product's demise. This was unfortunate as the Syndrum could actually be persuaded to sound very drum-like with judicious use of its controls. It was a very neat little unit, with an external brain and studio-type faders, and its pads actually featured tuneable plastic heads. Joe Pollard subsequently brought out a Mark II model which was cheaper and

Fig. 5.12

SIMMONS AMPLIFIER. SDC-200 amplifier. This unit was specially developed by Simmons as a compact, portable, amplification system, capable of handling the powerful range of sounds generated by an electronic drum kit.

easier to operate with integral controls.

At roughly the same time, on the East Coast of America, the company Star Inc. was involved in the research and development of synthesized drums. They too were looking on their product only as being an add-on to the normal set. The name of their product was Synare, and for a while was looked upon as being the only real alternative to Syndrum.

Another piece of electronic percussion equipment which made an early mark was the Moog percussion controller. It was launched around 1973 by Dr. R.A. Moog following the remarkable success of his synthesizers. Many keyboard players used to play this drum controller since it necessitated ownership of a (comparatively expensive) Minimoog - but consequently it never became a favourite of drummers.

The British weren't letting the grass grow under their feet at this time. Dave Simmons had begun his electronic drum experiments with a handful of triggers scavenged from keyboard synthesizers in the mid-Seventies. Simmons didn't actually produce a drum as such until 1978 when the SDS-3 was launched to critical acclaim. These drums were also meant as add-ons and bore very little relationship to the present Simmons product. They had wooden shells made by Premier, tuneable heads and a run generator to give the sound of several Toms from just one pad.

EARLY EDK
Early electronic drum kit brain.

In 1980 Simmons finally produced for the first time the actual sets which were to take the world by storm. At first customers and retailers alike were sceptical about this new solid bodied drum. It didn't even look like the Syndrum, Synare, or the Moog drum, which had only just begun to be grudgingly accepted. Glyn Thomas, a drummer who later became head of the US Simmons sales operation, vividly remembers the reaction he first encountered when introducing Simmons to the States. He was laughed out of the same New York music store which just a few months later gratefully accepted all the products he was prepared to allow it to have.

Simmons were the pioneers of the six-sided drum pad - the shape acting merely as an identifying trade mark. However, with their success came many imitators, and soon several companies were producing pads with that familiar hexagonal shape. In early 1985, Simmons company decided enough was enough. Their six-sided shape had been copied almost as much as Leo Fender's solid guitars, so they formally registered their shape as a trade mark. This effectively rendered several manufacturers' designs illegal, and forced them to rethink the shape of their pads.

The SDS electronic kits have evolved considerably since their introduction. The pads are no longer constructed with wood inside them and "riot-shield" plastic as the playing surface. They are now constructed completely of moulded ABS plastic with a stiffened rubber head which feels more like a drum. The SDS 9 was actually designed to sound and respond like a conventional acoustic drum with dynamic response curves carefully structured to achieve this.

There are many other revolutionary facilities to be found in the latest Simmons 'brains'. Besides the option of synthesized or digitally sampled sounds, computer generated voicing is also available. Mainland Europe too has recently turned its attention to electronic percussion, but the fruits are not primarily synthesizer based. They actually feature voices which have been computer sampled and subsequently 'blown' into an integrated chip. The Swedes have Ddrums, the Germans Dynachord, and the Dutch Digisound. All the companies specialise in full range sampled voices to a very high standard, and their pads are equally sophisticated.

The Japanese took a lot longer than expected to get involved in the building of electronic drums although they were more or less totally responsible, until very recently, for the bulk of the world's drum machines. Their first sets were very

SIMMONS SDS-7 Brain. All the electronics used to process the trigger information from the pads and to generate the percussion voices are housed in this device. Note that there are 12 channels. Into each channel a circuit card can be housed, thus enabling up to a 12 drum kit to be realised.

reminiscent of the Simmons design, but eventually, having established a market, they began to be more imaginative. Pearls, Tamas, Yamaha and Roland kits stand up on their own as being Hi-Tec state-of-the-art products.

A more recent development has been the use of pads to utilise the voices present in rhythm units. Casio, Simmons, and Roland have moved in this direction, with the MIDI link the obvious language of communication between controller and voices. Pads can be used either to play the voices in real time, or to load rhythm patterns into the drum machine, thus making the rhythm unit much more acceptable and accessible to the drummer.

The future would seem to be pulling the EDK manufacturers towards tuned percussion. This is obviously the next area destined for an electronic take-over bid.

ROLAND DRUM PADS. Used in conjunction with the DDR-30 brain.

CHAPTER 6
THE PLAYERS

A small, but significant band of drummers eagerly embraced the first electronic drum kits just as soon as they became available in the early Eighties. These were in the main high-profile players who had learnt their rudiments on acoustic drums, but who were ready to broaden their minds, and who weren't afraid of a little ridicule from their contemporaries. It should be said that at this time, even though there was a great deal of interest in electronic drums, very few were being sold.

One player who had something to do with the development of Simmons drums at the outset was Richard Burgess. He was the drummer with a progressive instrumental band called Landscape who subsequently went on to more salubrious pastures when he successfully produced Spandau Ballet. He was clearly responsible for turning on some of the so-called 'New Romantics' to the electronic possibilities offered by EDKs, and at this time they would have included a somewhat embryonic Duran Duran.

However, at the same time a much more revered 'drummers' drummer' was also enthusiastically experimenting with electronic percussion. Bill Bruford had played with several 'household' name bands and since his style was nothing if not 'avant garde', he was a natural for the new sounds and playing techniques demanded by electronics. He is still very much involved with these instruments and generally uses a 'hybrid' set, consisting of different Simmons products, as well as 'real' drums. He is the most innovative user and has been known to adapt his style and approach to enable a particular sound to fit into what he's playing. It would be fair to say that the sound is his inspiration.

Warren Cann too was an early convert to electronics with Ultravox, although his idea and concept of it is not so much to do with five pads and a 'brain'. He preferred to link synthesizers to his pads as well as drum machines, echoes and digital delays. He even used the odd 'ordinary' acoustic drum.

Michael Shrieve was for many years the drummer with Carlos Santana's band. He is, as you'd expect, an 'electric' set player these days, but he has the unique distinction of being one of the first pros to be seen with 'Impakt' drums back in the mid-Seventies. These were no doubt used to good effect with Automatic Man and later with Stomu Yamashta.

Sly Dunbar is the most famous of reggae drummers who uses electronic drums tastefully within the framework of the music he plays so well. His sparing use of single beat fills is ideal for the sort of long drum sounds which can be produced by an EDK. Phil Collins has a set of two of course even though the majority of his recorded drum sounds seem to consist of previously sampled sounds which have been loaded into some sort of sound retaining device (like AMS) which will spit them out when necessary. His co-drummer with Genesis is Chester Thompson who uses an electronic set on stage alongside his acoustic one, and this is something which many drummers playing with big name singers are beginning to do. Certainly Tony Brock with Rod Stewart and Charlie Morgan with Elton John have adopted this approach.

Some drummers are utilising electronics without actually being seen to do so. Many players have a 'brain' either on stage with them, or out at the mixing board where the engineer may 'tap' into it as and when he needs to extricate its more colourful sounds. 1985's biggest world-wide star has a drum sound which is instigated by his drummer's four drum acoustic set, but invariably it owes more to oscillators produced as bi-products of the 'space race' than it does to membranes stretched over wooden cylinders. More analogue than log you might say.

Any list of EDK users reads like a Who's Who of modern drumming. It would be simpler, and safer, to say who doesn't appear to be linked with the new technology. Even then the only one who immediately springs to mind is Buddy Rich. Mind you, even he must have given them the once over. Continuing in that vein it's safe to assume that very little if any 'cool' i.e. Modern Jazz has been played on an electric drum set. But, with the response and feel available there's no real reason why it couldn't. Max Roach, one of the leading lights in small-group jazz for the past two or three decades, has one so we shall see.

It's a 'moot point', but the first recorded instances of the Mark 2 EDKs (as opposed to Syndrum, Synare, and Moogdrum), were on records by Dave Stewart and Tom Dolby. But, without a shadow of a doubt, it was Bill Bruford who took their sound and their look to the masses in the 'live' situation.

EDKs For ALL?

These days, anyone who's anyone owns, or has access to, an electronic set as well as the obligatory acoustic one. If you're a professional you can't afford to lose a session/gig because you haven't the right equipment.

Many players are happy to rent their equipment because this enables them to keep up with the latest technological developments. Rental companies invariably purchase the new 'toys' immediately they become available; this enables them to be competitive. Some professionals operate a shared ownership scheme of the more up-market pieces of electronic drum equipment in order to cut down their initial outlay.

For many years keyboard players have had electric pianos and synthesizers within their armoury, so shouldn't drummers have both sorts of drum set?

CHAPTER 7
INTERVIEW

An Interview with Dave Simmons

Dave Simmons is the man to whom virtually all the credit is due for the development of the electronic drum kit. His company Simmons Electronics Ltd has been responsible for nearly all the recent developments in electronic percussion, and since the late Seventies has been the undisputed world market leader.

In what direction do you see electronic drum kits going from here?

It must be upwards and onwards. There's one main reason that electronic drums can only go onwards - the advance of technology. All electronic instruments have advanced with the relentless march of technological progress, but their acoustic counterparts can by definition really only stand still.

Do you see electronic drum kits becoming a lot more refined?

Yes, in terms of their playing I see them having all the refinements of the acoustic drum kit. I'm not sure whether we are going to go quite as far as the "damp thumb across the skin", but they will have all the major characteristics of their acoustic counterpart - rim shot, tuning, variable harmonics across the head etc. I even see them offering more "playing facilities" than the acoustic drum kit.

Do you think that electronic kits will become directed more towards the generation of abstract and sampled percussive sounds, or will they strive primarily to emulate the acoustic kit?

The SDS-9 is a mixture of everything we've done and as far as the playability is concerned things are definitely going to go the way of the SDS-9. And as far as the sound generation aspect is concerned, i.e. using sample sounds as a basis for analogue processing circuitry, things will progress a lot further in this direction but in a far more sophisticated manner. We're heading towards a new flagship instrument in 18 months or so, which will be a completely new instrument - it will still be drum based but as far as sound capability is concerned, it will be even better than the SDS-7.

How do you feel about incorporating a sequencer within the brain of the kit?

Every time you add something to a product, such as a sequencer, you increase the cost, and obviously people who don't want sequencers don't want to have to pay for one. So I think our policy will be to produce separate sequencers.

Do you see another pick-up system to the drum or do you think the piezo (a small pick-up that acts like a microphone mounted in the pad) **will continue to be utilised?**

We are investigating three different types of pick-up at the moment. The one thing you won't be seeing from Simmons is a pick-up system for acoustic drums. What we are investigating is a more complex playing head. I don't think you will see piezos carrying on for much longer. There are far better things around.

Will Simmons drums adopt a more "Hi-tech" image in the future?

Simmons has a big company image although we are basically still pretty small, and we realise now that the products we have don't have a particularly hi-tech image compared with, say, the Japanese. I think you'll see, from now on, Simmons products having a more hi-tech image; we are currently investing in the type of manufacturing equipment that is necessary to do that.

Nowadays many manufacturers are being criticised for making products that are difficult to use and which fail to provide the musician with sufficient visual information to let him know what is going to happen when he plays the instrument. In addition the incremental method of programming is considered to be slow and awkward to use. What are your feelings on this subject?
Consider the very successful synthesizer from Yamaha - the DX-7. Here you have a very clever computer controlled instrument with very limited display facilities - it's very difficult to see exactly what's happening, and slow and difficult to programme. Now if Yamaha had put individual controls for each parameter, such as say the old Prophet 5, it would probably double the price of the instrument. Displaying control information is a problem, especially with an instrument such as the DX-7 and SDS-7 that has the flexibility to change all the parameters. The easiest way to display things is to have a TV screen which can show whatever you want, but generally I don't think drummers like that either.

Actually at the moment "hi-tech" instruments are tending to rely less and less on displays. You may have one or two fluorescent displays or LCDs, but you don't have, what everyone would like to see, a knob with lights round the edge indicating its position. You could twiddle the knob and either use it visually or use your ear - but it would be very, very expensive. Hardware is always the problem. If you could develop a versatile fully programmable instrument that doesn't need to continually display a wide selection of information then you've got it.

So if your machines were totally digital and pre-set they would be considerably cheaper?
Yes, you can look around at the digital machines at the moment - Yamaha being a prime example - and now they've got a £250 retail digital drum machine. It's got very good voices but you can't tune them all individually, you don't have any bends, you don't have any filter on the voice, you're stuck with the voices they have chosen and that's a direct trade off between the versatility and the price. Everybody wants digital drum sounds for their portable studios and there it is for under £300. You can't argue with it but if you want to start messing around with it and you want to do some sophisticated manipulation of digital sounds then you have to start paying the price.

How do you feel about plagiarism? Simmons kits have been copied not only in terms of the sounds and electronics, but even in the shape of the pads - you've probably been as much ripped-off as Leo Fender was over the years.
Well, we have managed to defend ourselves quite successfully against both Tama and Pearl and we have managed to force them to change the shape of their pads and really that's been our only strength. We can't defend ourselves on the electronic side, even though every analogue kit that comes out has the controls that I first defined five years ago. But where I did get angry was with the image . . . one Japanese company, for example . . . the way they were advertising and selling it, and even the type of environment they were promoting their kit in was a direct rip-off of our image. They were most definitely selling off our backs and that's where we said, if we let that sort of thing go, we would be flooded by instruments that looked and sounded just like ours. So we fought on the shape of the drums and we won worldwide.

What was it do you think that eventually made the electronic drum kit take off?
The image of the thing and some very basic features, such as the tom toms, pulled in everything behind it. It was a way of getting some exciting new sounds and a new way to use drums and yet maybe it wasn't the drummers who picked up on it. I think it was probably the producers.

Did you envisage, having made the SDS-3 back in the late Seventies, that you would be in this position some six years later?
Yes, I think so. I think you always have to have that vision, otherwise you wouldn't get on with it. Whatever stage you are at you've got to say, "Do I take my money and run, or do I plough it back into expanding the business?" We've done the latter and so far it's worked.

APPENDIX I

Synchronising and Interfacing Electronic Percussion Instruments

This section deals with the use of the rhythm machine in conjunction with other electronic devices.

Using electronic percussion is all about creating a beat, but that would be pointless if the other rhythmic parts of your music were not kept in time.

Unlike human drummers, drum machines are incapable of simply listening to the other musicians and playing along. If you want to add a percussion track to an existing piece of music then it has to be electronically locked in to the tempo of the music. There are several ways of doing this.

These methods are applied in one of two ways - by locking the drum machine to the tempo of the music, or by locking the music to the tempo of the drum machine. Both procedures are widely used in recording and live performance alike.

In addition to such "synchronisation", most drum machines have facilities either for individual audio amplification of sounds, or for external triggering, trigger output, sampling, information exchange or any combination of these. Since synchronisation is the most important facility in relation to using drum machines with other electronic instruments, we'll look at this function first.

Synchronisation

There are six basic methods of synchronizing drum machines to other equipment.

a) Tape Sync.
b) Clock Pulses.
c) Sync 24.
d) Sync 48.
e) MIDI.
f) SMPTE.

Several products now on the market will convert from one of these standards to another, but the original major applications for each of them are as stated below.

a) Tape Sync
Most drum machines are capable of generating a series of pulses when playing which can be recorded on to tape. When these are replayed into the drum machine its internal clock and tempo control will be over-ridden in favour of the tempo dictated by the tape pulses. See *Fig. 8.01*.

The advantages of using this system are enormous. If the tape signal is recorded on just one track of a multi-track tape machine, the drum part can be altered, added to, edited or re-recorded in perfect synchronization at any stage by using the tape sync facility. If other units such as sequencers can be locked in, either directly to the tape signal or to the drum machine as it is being run by the signal, then they too can be added, edited and overdubbed at will.

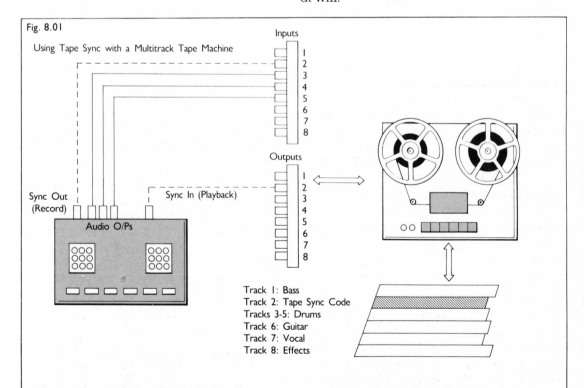

Fig. 8.01

Using Tape Sync with a Multitrack Tape Machine

Inputs
1
2
3
4
5
6
7
8

Outputs
1
2
3
4
5
6
7
8

Sync Out (Record)

Sync In (Playback)

Audio O/Ps

Track 1: Bass
Track 2: Tape Sync Code
Tracks 3-5: Drums
Track 6: Guitar
Track 7: Vocal
Track 8: Effects

The Tape Sync Code is recorded on Track 2 along with the drums on Tracks 3-5 or the Bass on Track 1. Subsequently the drums can be changed, erased or added to without losing synchronization with other parts by using Tape Sync In during Playback. Alternatively the drum parts can be left off the multitrack (saving valuable tracks) and mixed directly on to the master in perfect synchronisation.

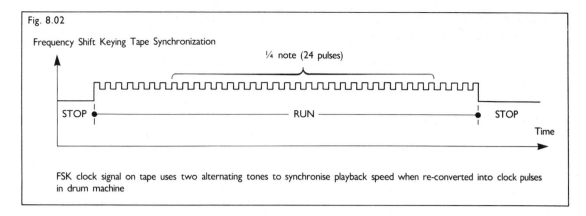

Fig. 8.02

Frequency Shift Keying Tape Synchronization

¼ note (24 pulses)

STOP — RUN — STOP

Time

FSK clock signal on tape uses two alternating tones to synchronise playback speed when re-converted into clock pulses in drum machine

There are several types of tape sync signal which are often incompatible with one another, but luckily it's unusual to want to drive one drum machine off the tape sync signal of another machine. The most common method used, however, is Frequency Shift Keying, or FSK, which involves the generation of a tone rapidly varying in pitch (often sounding like a warbling telephone) which varies according to the tempo of the drum machine.

Since tempo may vary from 40 to 240 Beats Per Minute in normal use, the FSK method has been chosen for its ability to maintain synchronization over this very wide range. *Fig. 8.02* illustrates the FSK principles.

Tape Sync signals are generally very reliable as long as they are recorded at a sufficiently high level, and there are no drop-outs or clicks on the tape. Most drum machines generate a steady tone from the Tape Sync socket while stopped which allows you to set the recording level for the sync signal. Generally this is around 0 VU.

Many products now exist to produce tape sync signals from other types of pulse, and so it is usually possible to add tape sync to a drum machine which does not have the feature as standard. Examples of such units include the MPC SYNC TRAK and the KORG (Unicord) KMS-30.

Increasingly tape sync is used to run a drum machine "live" into the final mix - this frees many tracks of tape and allows every audio output of the drum machine to be individually treated and equalised on the mixer.

b) Clock Pulses

Clock Pulses are used to synchronise drum machines to one another, to sequencers and to other instruments. The typical clock pulse is fairly straightforward - a momentary level of about 5 volts lasting perhaps 100 milliseconds and delivered 24, 48 or 96 times for every quarter note played by the drum machine.

Clock pulses aren't suitable for recording on tape (since tape will not reliably return the correct voltage) but like FSK signals can operate over a wide tempo range.

Some drum machines are capable of responding to a selection of clock pulse rates while others are permanently set at one rate, and clearly the latter type of unit may respond at half or double the required speed if used with machines of other standards.

Clock signals are used if two drum machines are to be run together, or if a drum machine is to be used to run a sequencer or vice-versa. Many drum machines can produce a clock out but cannot accept a clock in, and so always have to be used as the driving unit in such a set-up. On machines which do have a Clock In function, the socket used is often that used for loading information from cassette as well (see Information Exchange).

Some clock rate examples:

Unit	Rate (Pulses per ¼ note, ppqn)
Oberheim	★ 96
LinnDrum	★ 48
Drumtraks	★ 24/48/96
Drumulator	★ 24
MXR Drum	★ 24

Several units now exist to convert clock rates thus increasing the compatibility of any particular machine.

c) Sync 24

This refers to a synchronization method introduced on the early ROLAND drum machines and subsequently used by many other manufacturers. It takes the form of a five pin, 180 degree DIN socket of which only three pins are actually connected (see *Fig. 8.03*).

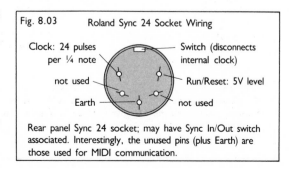

Fig. 8.03   Roland Sync 24 Socket Wiring

Clock: 24 pulses per ¼ note — Switch (disconnects internal clock)

not used — Run/Reset: 5V level

Earth — not used

Rear panel Sync 24 socket; may have Sync In/Out switch associated. Interestingly, the unused pins (plus Earth) are those used for MIDI communication.

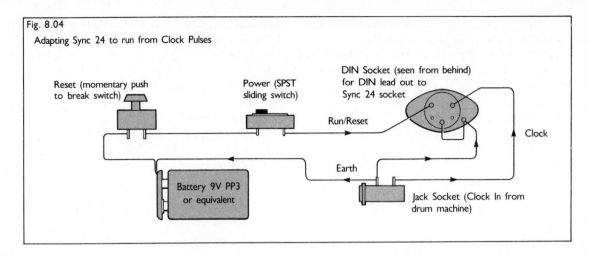

Fig. 8.04

Adapting Sync 24 to run from Clock Pulses

Reset (momentary push to break switch)

Power (SPST sliding switch)

DIN Socket (seen from behind) for DIN lead out to Sync 24 socket

Run/Reset

Clock

Earth

Battery 9V PP3 or equivalent

Jack Socket (Clock In from drum machine)

One of the connected pins is an earth, another carries a constant clock signal (whether the unit is running or not) of 24 pulses per quarter note, and the third pin carries a Run/Reset signal. This is held at an approximate 5 volt level for Run, and when this level falls to zero the unit stops and resets itself to the start of the current pattern or song.

By connecting a suitable battery across the earth and Run/Reset terminals of a Sync 24 input socket it's possible to operate the unit from a simple 24 pulse per quarter note clock signal, although the Reset function will of course be lost (see *Fig. 8.04*).

Some units have separate In and Out Sync 24 sockets, while others have a single socket and an In/Out Selector switch.

Sync 24 can be used to synchronise drum machines to each other or to sequencers and other equipment, and the standard is now common on computer interfaces, clock dividers and other units. Thanks to the various converters on the market, the clock part of the Sync 24 signal can also be converted to Tape Sync usage, adding this facility to many drum machines which do not have it.

d) Sync 48

An arbitrary name for KORG's (Unicord's) preferred method of synchronization. Identical to the ROLAND Sync 24 system in every respect save that it uses 48 pulses per quarter note, the system appears on all of KORG's drum machines and on several of their sequencers and other units.

KORG market a converter unit, the KMS-30 which can adapt Sync 48 signals to Tape Sync usage and also convert Sync 24 to Sync 48 and vice-versa. Should you ever want to write slow drum or sequencer patterns which are twice as long as is normally possible (in relation to other instrumental parts playing at the same time) this unit may provide the solution.

e) MIDI

MIDI (Musical Instrument Digital Interface) is the most advanced form of synchronization commonly available, but its introduction was accompanied by much confusion, particularly on the question of tempo synchronization.

In fact the MIDI clock signal is simply 24 pulses per quarter note, but these pulses are not in the same form as Clock or Sync 24 pulses and cannot even be dealt with in isolation without a good deal of digital manipulation.

This is due to the "serial" nature of data transmitted over MIDI. Information is sent one piece at a time and that information on different subjects may be interleaved. This is in fact what happens with clock information, in between the clock pulses there may be information on what keys are being played on a synthesizer, what pattern number should be playing, and even what model of instrument is sending the information. See *Fig. 8.05*.

Fig. 8.05

MIDI Codes for Tempo Synchronization

MIDI System Real Time codes are intended for all channels and should be responded to by all relevant instruments. Time codes are interleaved with other information, except System Exclusive (used for data dump etc.).

MIDI 1.0 differs from OLD MIDI, but all Real Time codes still consist of a single byte (8-digit binary number) starting with a 1. Codes now used are:

1 ★★★/★★★★ = 248	Clock Pulse
= 250	Start
= 252	Stop
= 255	Reset

For example,   1111/1100 = 252 = Stop

or   1111/1000 = 248 = Clock Pulse

In Play, 1111/1000 is transmitted 24 times per quarter note.

The clock pulse itself is a digital binary code set at low voltage levels for interpretation by a microprocessor, and so even if it is extracted from the stream of MIDI information it remains incompatible with Clock and Sync 24 pulses.

However, units from KORG and GARFIELD do exist which can receive a MIDI signal containing a clock, carry out the necessary digital interpretation and re-transmit a Sync 24, Sync 48 or assortment of clock pulses as appropriate.

f) SMPTE

The timing standard of the Society of Motion Picture and Television Engineers, (SMPTE) has until recently been expensive to implement and so rarely used outside film and TV studios. But audio-visual studios needing to lock electronic instruments to film or video for advertising jingles, soundtracks and other applications provided a market for cheaper SMPTE-reading equipment, and this is now becoming widely available.

SMPTE is more complex than other codes as it is a complete time code, containing information on hour, minute, second and frame number at the rate of 25-31 frames per second (there are several variations on the basic SMPTE standard). The system is even capable of transmitting the day and the month, although this wouldn't be of much use to the average drum machine. *Fig. 8.06* shows diagrammatically the form of the SMPTE code.

Machines having SMPTE fitted as standard or as an option include the LINN 9000 and the E-MU EMULATOR SP12. SMPTE is also available on the E-MU EMULATOR 2 keyboard, which has many percussion applications, and on sync boxes such as the SBX-80 (*Fig. 8.07* from ROLAND).

The SBX-80 lays down and reads SMPTE code and sends out more familiar codes such as Sync 24 and clock pulses as well. This allows virtually any drum machine to gain at least some of the benefits of SMPTE, although there are few which can take advantage of all its capabilities - such as allowing a drum machine to drop in at the right bar of a song no matter where the tape is started.

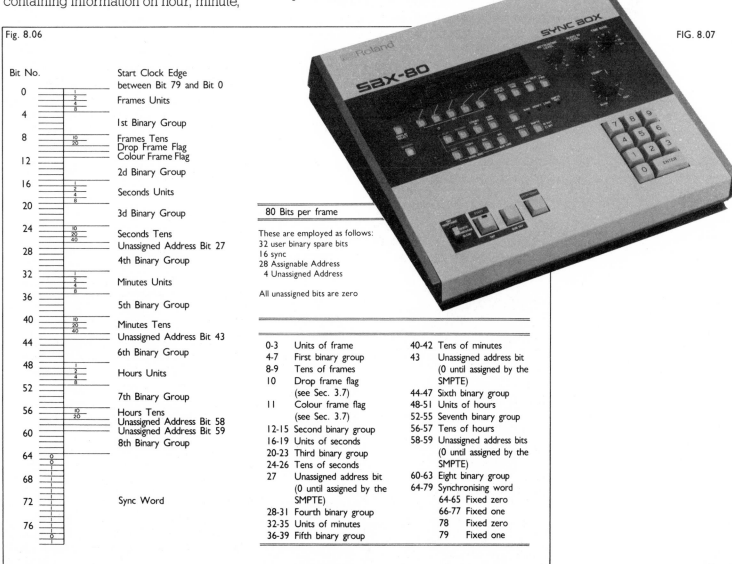

Fig. 8.06

FIG. 8.07

Bit No.		Start Clock Edge between Bit 79 and Bit 0
0	1 2 4 8	Frames Units
4		1st Binary Group
8	10 20	Frames Tens
		Drop Frame Flag
		Colour Frame Flag
12		2d Binary Group
16	1 2 4 8	Seconds Units
20		3d Binary Group
24	10 20 40	Seconds Tens
		Unassigned Address Bit 27
28		4th Binary Group
32	1 2 4 8	Minutes Units
36		5th Binary Group
40	10 20 40	Minutes Tens
		Unassigned Address Bit 43
44		6th Binary Group
48	1 2 4 8	Hours Units
52		7th Binary Group
56	10 20	Hours Tens
		Unassigned Address Bit 58
60		Unassigned Address Bit 59
		8th Binary Group
64		
68		
72		Sync Word
76		

80 Bits per frame

These are employed as follows:
32 user binary spare bits
16 sync
28 Assignable Address
 4 Unassigned Address

All unassigned bits are zero

0-3	Units of frame	40-42	Tens of minutes
4-7	First binary group	43	Unassigned address bit
8-9	Tens of frames		(0 until assigned by the
10	Drop frame flag		SMPTE)
	(see Sec. 3.7)	44-47	Sixth binary group
11	Colour frame flag	48-51	Units of hours
	(see Sec. 3.7)	52-55	Seventh binary group
12-15	Second binary group	56-57	Tens of hours
16-19	Units of seconds	58-59	Unassigned address bits
20-23	Third binary group		(0 until assigned by the
24-26	Tens of seconds		SMPTE)
27	Unassigned address bit	60-63	Eight binary group
	(0 until assigned by the	64-79	Synchronising word
	SMPTE)		64-65 Fixed zero
28-31	Fourth binary group		66-77 Fixed one
32-35	Units of minutes		78 Fixed zero
36-39	Fifth binary group		79 Fixed one

Audio Outputs

Drum machines, as distinct from most synthesizers, produce many different sounds simultaneously, and when performing or recording with these sounds they often need to be treated in different ways.

This is next to impossible when all the sounds come out of a single audio output socket, but luckily all but the most basic drum machines have multiple audio outputs.

Ideally a drum machine would have one audio output for every sound which can be played, but since this is an expensive proposition most popular units make a compromise. Sounds are arranged in sets which are likely to need similar treatment at any given time, and each set of sounds has its own audio output.

The SCI DRUMTRAKS, for instance, has 13 sounds but only six audio outputs (in addition to a total Mix Output). The Bass Drum is on Channel 1, the Snare Drum and Rimshot on Channel 2, the two Toms on Channel 3, the Crash and Ride cymbals on Channel 4, the Open and Closed Hi-Hat sounds on Channel 5, and the four Percussion sounds on Channel 6.

This allows all the most important audio treatments to be carried out at the mixing desk. The bass drum can be equalised for a deep, powerful sound, and the snare drum's tone can be accurately set. Some reverb or echo can be added to the snare, but this would affect the rimshot as well since the two share a channel. The Toms can be equalised, but only in the same way - any reverb or echo used will affect both, and it's not possible to pan the toms apart in stereo, and so on.

One solution to the problems of shared outputs is to move the EPROM chips within the machine to different sockets so that the sounds appear from different audio output channels. For instance, if on the DRUMTRAKS you want a powerful dry tom sound on the right and a thinner reverbed tom on the left, you could substitute a tom chip in the percussion slot so that one tom sound emerges from Channel 3 and the other from Channel 6, allowing different treatments and panning to be used.

Some machines such as the SCI TOM have only two audio outputs. Often these are used to give a fixed stereo spread of the drum sounds, but on the TOM the stereo position of each instrument is programmable and variable within a pattern.

Potentially at least, this means that you could pan the Snare sound to one output for treatment with a reverb, while all the other sounds would come out of the other

output and would be treated in the same way.

Some drum machines which lack individual audio outputs, such as the ROLAND TR606 and KORG (Unicord) DDM110/220 can have these added fairly easily by any service centre (this will void your warranty however). Others generate all their sounds from one chip so it's not possible to provide separate outputs. Examples include the computer-based SYNTRON DIGIDRUM.

Trigger Inputs

Drum machines usually set out to imitate acoustic drum kits, but often it's desirable to play the drum sounds by hand to obtain a more realistic "feel". Most digital drum machines have pads which allow you to tap out a single drum sound, but often these aren't very satisfactory for precise playing.

The ability to connect a drum-like pad would help, and many machines have one or more sockets to make this possible. Usually a pad such as those marketed by SIMMONS, containing a piezo crystal which gives a pulse when struck, is suitable.

Trigger input facilities vary greatly from one machine to another. Some have a trigger input socket for every sound; others have only four or five inputs which can be programmed to control any selection of sounds such as on the E-MU DRUMULATOR.

Some machines such as the HAMMOND DPM 48 (SAKATA) use a multi-pin socket which connects to an interface allowing pads to trigger any of its sounds.

Trigger inputs can also allow you to control your drum machine from another drum machine's trigger outputs, from a sequencer or other unit.

Usually the presence of trigger inputs will allow you to program patterns from a set of pads, often with dynamics. This can make your drum machine much more life-like in the recording studio.

Some products now exist which will reproduce the function of trigger inputs over MIDI. This allows you to interface, for example, a SIMMONS drum kit to any MIDI drum machine with dynamics, patch changes and so on. One such product is the PERCUSSION SIGNAL PROCESSOR.

Trigger Outputs

Not to be confused with clock outputs, a trigger output derives from only one particular sound, and a trigger occurs only when that sound operates.

There may be only one trigger output on a drum machine - the DR-110 DR RHYTHM GRAPHIC from ROLAND produces a trigger on every beat which has an Accent programmed - while on the ROLAND TR-606 there are two trigger outputs referring to the High and Low Tom sounds. These make it possible to set up an alternative sound on a synth or digital drum module, turn down the level of the original sound and so accurately replace it whenever it occurs.

Larger machines offer more trigger outputs - the ROLAND TR-808 has trigger outputs from Bass, Accent and Clap - and ideally every sound should have a trigger output so that it can be replaced by sounds generated externally if desired. This is a relatively simple modification on the TR-606.

Sometimes the uses of Trigger Outputs and Audio Outputs overlap. Particularly when short sounds such as Cowbell or Rimshot are used, an Audio Output can be capable of driving a Trigger Input if its level is sufficiently high. On some synthesizers, such as the SCI Pro One, an onboard sequencer can be stepped from almost any drum machine clock, metronome or audio output.

Metronome

Most digital drum machines which are programmed in Real Time generate a metronome beat with which the programmer can play along. Often this is available at a separate socket, either to amplify it above the sound of other musicians, or to record it on a spare track of tape for later use.

Since the metronome plays single pulses on the beat (3/4, 4/4 etc.) rather than 24, 48 or 96 pulses per quarter note, it can be useful for stepping sequencers and other units too. If the level is too low for this purpose it can often be boosted on the mixing desk. The metronome facility is a good way of interfacing older analogue equipment such as sequencers with newer digital drum machines.

Keep in mind that on some machines, the metronome will occur only while in Record mode.

Sampling Inputs

Many digital drum machines use sounds sampled at the factory from acoustic instruments, but there are now a few units which can sample sounds for the end user and record them on disc or tape.

These include the LINN 9008 and the E-MU EMULATOR SP-12. Usually the sampling socket is a standard jack with switchable level to cope with microphone or line inputs, and the drum machine has some kind of input level display to ensure

a distortion-free sample. On the EMULATOR SP-12 this is one of the many modes of the LCD display, which converts into a VU ladder for the purpose.

Once a sample has been taken it is stored on disc or tape, or permanently "blown" on to a chip using an EPROM burner.

Information Exchange

Most digital drum machines are capable of coding the contents of their memories on to tape, allowing you to build up a library of songs and patterns on cassette.

The user simply connects the Tape Out jack to a cassette player, presses Save and records the resulting tones. These can be checked against the contents of the memory (Verify) and reloaded at any time (Load).

While this system is reliable given clean tape heads and good quality cassettes it can be slow to use and is not recommended for use on stage.

The MIDI socket on most digital drum machines is also capable of sending pattern, song and even sound information in the specialised mode known as System Exclusive. This section of the MIDI standard allows manufacturers to configure information in any manner convenient to them, for the exchange of specialised information between units of their own manufacture.

For instance, it's possible to perform a MIDI Data Dump from one drum machine's memory into the empty memory of another. Of course this is also possible using tape, but the MIDI method is much faster and more reliable.

On machines which make and store their own samples it's possible to send sound data along the MIDI bus in System Exclusive mode as well. Eventually there may be an agreement covering the digital coding of sound samples which would make it possible to transfer sounds from one machine to another of a different make. When this is the case, many of the problems of synchronization and incompatibility will vanish - you will always be able to use whatever machine you're most comfortable with to obtain the sound you need.

APPENDIX 3

Percussion

Over the next few pages are listed various rhythm patterns which can be loaded into most rhythm units, or if you are using an electronic kit that utilises MIDI, then the patterns can be recorded into a sequencer and used to drive the kit.

The patterns are written in a matrix format with a number indicating where in the pattern each note falls. This has been found to be the clearest way of denoting a pattern, and faster for entering the pattern in step time. These patterns are merely guidelines for you to experiment with. Not all patterns will work with all machines, for example certain rhythm units may not be able to accommodate 20 step patterns.

The voicings given is also just a guide — you can of course change the instrumentation to suit your particular drum machine — if for example your unit is not equipped with Conga voices (say), then you can normally get away with using Toms.

A space has been provided under each pattern for notes to be made relating to that pattern for future reference.

We would like to thank YAMAHA, ROLAND and KORG for giving us permission to use some of the patterns they have developed for their individual drum machines, in this section.

4 BEAT — 12 STEPS

INSTRUMENT	1	2	3	4	5	6	7	8	9	10	11	12
C. HI-HAT	·	·	·	4	·	6	·	·	·	10	·	12
O. HI-HAT	1	·	·	·	·	·	7	·	·	·	·	·
SNARE DRUM	·	·	·	·	·	·	·	·	·	·	·	12
BASS DRUM	1	·	·	·	·	·	·	·	·	·	·	·
ACCENT	1	·	·	4	·	·	7	·	·	10	·	·
CYMBAL	1	·	·	4	·	·	7	·	·	10	·	·
HANDCLAP	·	·	·	4	·	·	·	·	·	10	·	·

NOTES SWING

ROCK 1 — (8 BEAT) 16 STEPS

INSTRUMENT	1	2	3	4	5	6	7	8	9	10	11	12	13	14	15	16
C. HI-HAT	·	·	·	·	·	·	·	·	·	·	·	·	·	·	·	·
O. HI-HAT	·	·	·	·	·	·	·	·	·	·	·	·	·	·	·	·
SNARE DRUM	·	·	·	·	5	·	·	·	·	·	·	·	13	·	·	·
BASS DRUM	1	·	·	·	·	·	·	·	9	·	11	·	·	·	·	·
ACCENT	1	·	·	·	5	·	·	·	9	·	·	·	13	·	·	·
CYMBAL	1	·	3	·	5	·	7	·	9	·	11	·	13	·	15	·
HANDCLAP	·	·	·	·	·	·	·	·	·	·	·	·	·	·	·	·

NOTES

8 BEAT I — 16 STEPS

INSTRUMENT	1	2	3	4	5	6	7	8	9	10	11	12	13	14	15	16
C. HI-HAT	1	·	3	·	5	·	7	·	9	·	11	·	13	·	15	·
SNARE DRUM	·	·	·	·	5	·	·	·	·	·	·	·	13	·	·	·
BASS DRUM	1	·	·	·	·	·	7	·	9	·	·	·	·	·	·	·
ACCENT	1	·	·	·	5	·	·	·	9	·	·	·	13	·	·	·

NOTES

8 BEAT II — 16 STEPS

INSTRUMENT	1	2	3	4	5	6	7	8	9	10	11	12	13	14	15	16
C. HI-HAT	1	·	3	·	5	·	7	·	9	·	11	·	13	·	15	·
SNARE DRUM	·	·	·	·	5	·	·	·	·	·	·	·	13	·	·	·
BASS DRUM	1	·	3	·	·	·	·	8	·	10	11	·	·	·	·	·
ACCENT	1	·	·	·	5	·	·	·	9	·	·	·	13	·	·	·

NOTES

8 BEAT III — 16 STEPS

INSTRUMENT	1	2	3	4	5	6	7	8	9	10	11	12	13	14	15	16
O. HI-HAT	·	·	·	·	·	·	·	·	·	·	11	·	·	·	·	·
C. HI-HAT	1	·	3	·	5	·	7	·	9	·	·	·	13	·	15	·
SNARE DRUM	·	·	·	·	5	·	·	·	·	·	·	·	13	·	·	·
BASS DRUM	·	·	3	·	·	6	·	·	9	·	·	·	·	·	·	·
ACCENT	1	·	·	·	5	·	·	·	9	·	·	·	13	·	·	·

NOTES Good basic Rock Funk

8 BEAT IV — 16 STEPS

INSTRUMENT	1	2	3	4	5	6	7	8	9	10	11	12	13	14	15	16
O. HI-HAT	·	·	3	·	·	·	·	·	·	·	11	·	·	·	·	·
C. HI-HAT	1	·	·	·	·	·	7	8	9	10	·	·	13	·	15	·
SNARE DRUM	·	·	·	·	5	·	·	·	·	·	·	·	13	·	·	·
BASS DRUM	1	·	·	·	·	·	·	·	·	·	11	·	·	14	·	·
ACCENT	1	·	·	·	5	·	·	·	·	·	·	·	13	·	·	·

NOTES Funk type beat

8 BEAT V — 16 STEPS

INSTRUMENT	1	2	3	4	5	6	7	8	9	10	11	12	13	14	15	16
C. HI-HAT	1	·	3	·	5	·	7	·	9	·	11	·	13	·	15	·
SNARE DRUM	·	2	·	·	5	·	·	8	·	10	·	·	13	·	·	16
BASS DRUM	1	·	·	4	·	6	·	·	9	·	·	12	·	14	·	·

NOTES

8 BEAT VI — 16 STEPS

INSTRUMENT	1	2	3	4	5	6	7	8	9	10	11	12	13	14	15	16
C. HI-HAT	1	·	3	·	5	·	7	·	9	·	11	·	13	·	15	·
SNARE DRUM	·	2	·	·	5	·	·	8	·	·	11	·	·	14	·	·
BASS DRUM	·	·	·	4	·	6	·	·	·	10	·	12	·	·	·	16

NOTES

8 BEAT VII — 16 STEPS

INSTRUMENT	1	2	3	4	5	6	7	8	9	10	11	12	13	14	15	16
C. HI-HAT	1	·	3	·	5	·	7	·	9	·	11	·	13	·	15	·
SNARE DRUM	·	·	·	·	5	·	·	·	·	10	·	·	13	·	·	·
BASS DRUM	1	·	3	4	·	·	·	8	·	·	·	12	·	14	·	16

NOTES

8 BEAT SHUFFLE — 24 STEPS

INSTRUMENT	1	2	3	4	5	6	7	8	9	10	11	12	1	2	3	4	5	6	7	8	9	10	11	12
C. HI-HAT	1	·	·	4	·	·	7	·	·	10	·	·	1	·	·	4	·	·	7	·	·	10	·	·
SNARE DRUM	·	·	·	4	·	·	·	·	·	10	·	·	·	·	·	4	·	·	·	·	·	10	·	·
BASS DRUM	1	·	·	·	·	·	7	·	9	·	·	12	·	·	3	·	·	·	7	·	9	·	·	·
ACCENT	·	·	·	4	·	·	·	·	·	10	·	·	·	·	·	4	·	·	·	·	·	10	·	·

NOTES

8 BEAT BOUNCE — 24 STEPS

INSTRUMENT	1	2	3	4	5	6	7	8	9	10	11	12	1	2	3	4	5	6	7	8	9	10	11	12
C. HI-HAT	1	·	·	4	·	·	7	·	·	10	·	·	1	·	·	4	·	·	7	·	·	10	·	·
SNARE DRUM	·	·	·	·	·	·	7	·	·	·	·	·	·	·	3	·	·	·	·	·	·	·	·	·
BASS DRUM	1	·	·	·	·	6	·	·	·	·	·	12	1	·	·	·	·	6	·	·	·	·	·	12

NOTES

8 BEAT SLOW — 24 STEPS

INSTRUMENT	1	2	3	4	5	6	7	8	9	10	11	12	1	2	3	4	5	6	7	8	9	10	11	12
C. HI-HAT	1	·	·	4	·	·	7	·	·	10	·	·	1	·	·	4	·	·	7	·	·	10	·	·
SNARE DRUM	·	·	·	·	·	·	7	·	·	·	·	·	·	·	·	·	·	·	7	·	·	·	·	·
BASS DRUM	1	·	·	4	·	·	·	·	·	·	·	12	1	·	·	4	·	·	·	·	·	·	·	·

NOTES

16 BEAT — 16 STEPS

INSTRUMENT	1	2	3	4	5	6	7	8	9	10	11	12	13	14	15	16
C. HI-HAT	1	2	3	4	5	6	7	8	9	10	11	12	13	14	15	16
O. HI-HAT	·	·	·	·	5	·	·	·	9	·	·	·	13	·	·	·
SNARE DRUM	·	·	·	·	5	·	·	·	·	·	·	·	13	·	·	·
BASS DRUM	1	·	·	4	·	·	7	·	·	·	11	·	·	14	·	·
ACCENT	1	·	·	·	5	·	·	·	9	·	·	·	13	·	·	·
CYMBAL	1	·	3	4	5	·	7	8	9	·	11	12	13	·	15	16
HANDCLAP	·	·	·	·	·	·	·	·	·	·	·	·	·	·	·	·

NOTES Good Funk

16 BEAT I — 16 STEPS

INSTRUMENT	1	2	3	4	5	6	7	8	9	10	11	12	13	14	15	16
C. HI-HAT	1	2	3	4	5	6	7	8	9	10	11	12	13	14	15	16
SNARE DRUM	·	·	·	·	5	·	·	·	·	·	·	·	13	·	·	·
BASS DRUM	1	·	·	·	·	·	·	8	9	·	·	·	·	·	·	·
ACCENT	1	·	·	·	5	·	·	·	9	·	·	·	13	·	·	·

NOTES

16 BEAT II — 16 STEPS

INSTRUMENT	1	2	3	4	5	6	7	8	9	10	11	12	13	14	15	16
C. HI-HAT	1	2	3	4	5	6	7	8	9	10	11	12	13	14	15	16
SNARE DRUM	·	·	·	·	5	·	·	·	·	·	·	·	13	·	·	·
BASS DRUM	1	·	·	4	·	·	7	·	9	·	·	·	·	·	·	16
ACCENT	1	·	·	·	5	·	·	·	9	·	·	·	13	·	·	·

NOTES Good Funk

16 BEAT III — 16 STEPS

INSTRUMENT	1	2	3	4	5	6	7	8	9	10	11	12	13	14	15	16
O. HI-HAT	·	·	·	·	·	·	·	·	·	·	11	·	·	·	·	·
C. HI-HAT	1	2	3	4	5	6	7	8	9	10	·	12	13	14	15	16
SNARE DRUM	·	·	·	·	5	·	·	·	·	·	·	·	13	·	·	·
BASS DRUM	1	·	3	4	·	·	·	8	9	·	11	·	·	14	·	16
ACCENT	1	·	·	·	5	·	·	·	9	·	·	·	13	·	·	·

NOTES OK

16 BEAT IV — 16 STEPS

INSTRUMENT	1	2	3	4	5	6	7	8	9	10	11	12	13	14	15	16
O. HI-HAT	·	·	·	·	·	·	·	·	·	·	·	·	·	·	·	16
C. HI-HAT	1	2	3	4	5	6	7	8	9	10	11	12	13	14	15	·
SNARE DRUM	·	·	·	·	5	·	·	·	·	·	·	·	13	·	·	·
BASS DRUM	1	·	3	·	·	6	·	·	9	·	·	·	·	·	·	16
ACCENT	1	·	3	·	5	·	7	·	9	·	11	·	13	·	15	·

NOTES OK

16 BEAT V — 16 STEPS

INSTRUMENT	1	2	3	4	5	6	7	8	9	10	11	12	13	14	15	16
O. HI-HAT	·	·	·	·	·	·	·	·	·	·	·	·	·	·	15	·
C. HI-HAT	1	2	3	4	5	6	7	8	9	10	11	12	13	14	·	·
SNARE DRUM	·	·	·	·	5	·	·	·	·	·	·	·	13	·	·	·
TOM 3	·	·	·	·	·	·	·	·	·	·	·	·	·	·	15	·
BASS DRUM	1	·	·	·	·	·	·	8	9	·	·	·	·	·	·	·
ACCENT	·	·	3	·	·	6	·	·	9	·	·	12	·	·	·	·

NOTES

16 BEAT VI — 16 STEPS

INSTRUMENT	1	2	3	4	5	6	7	8	9	10	11	12	13	14	15	16
O. HI-HAT	·	·	3	·	·	·	·	·	9	·	·	·	·	·	·	·
C. HI-HAT	1	2	·	·	5	6	7	8	·	·	11	·	·	14	·	16
SNARE DRUM	·	·	·	·	5	·	·	·	·	·	·	·	13	·	·	·
TOM 2	·	·	·	·	·	·	·	·	·	·	·	12	·	·	·	·
TOM 3	·	·	·	·	·	·	·	·	·	·	·	·	·	·	15	·
BASS DRUM	1	·	·	·	·	·	7	·	9	·	·	·	·	·	·	·
ACCENT	·	·	·	·	5	·	·	·	·	·	·	·	·	·	·	16

NOTES OK

16 BEAT VII — 16 STEPS

INSTRUMENT	1	2	3	4	5	6	7	8	9	10	11	12	13	14	15	16
C. HI-HAT	1	2	3	4	5	6	7	8	9	10	11	12	13	14	15	16
SNARE DRUM	·	·	·	·	5	·	·	·	·	·	·	·	13	·	·	·
BASS DRUM	1	·	3	4	·	·	·	8	·	10	·	12	·	·	·	·
ACCENT	·	·	·	·	·	·	·	8	·	10	·	·	·	·	·	·

NOTES

16 BEAT VIII — 16 STEPS

INSTRUMENT	1	2	3	4	5	6	7	8	9	10	11	12	13	14	15	16
C. HI-HAT	1	2	3	4	5	6	7	8	9	10	11	12	13	14	15	16
SNARE DRUM	·	·	·	·	5	·	·	·	·	·	·	·	13	·	·	·
BASS DRUM	1	·	·	4	·	·	·	·	9	·	·	12	·	·	15	·
ACCENT	·	·	3	·	·	·	7	·	·	·	11	·	·	·	15	·

NOTES

16 BEAT IX — 16 STEPS

INSTRUMENT	1	2	3	4	5	6	7	8	9	10	11	12	13	14	15	16
O. HI-HAT	·	·	·	·	·	·	·	·	·	·	·	·	·	14	·	16
C. HI-HAT	1	2	3	4	·	·	7	8	9	10	11	12	·	·	15	·
SNARE DRUM	·	·	·	·	5	·	·	·	·	·	·	·	13	·	·	·
BASS DRUM	1	·	·	·	5	·	·	·	9	·	·	·	13	·	·	·

NOTES

16 BEAT X — 16 STEPS

INSTRUMENT	1	2	3	4	5	6	7	8	9	10	11	12	13	14	15	16
O. HI-HAT	·	·	3	·	·	·	7	8	·	·	11	·	·	·	15	16
C. HI-HAT	1	2	·	·	5	6	·	·	9	10	·	·	13	14	·	·
SNARE DRUM	·	·	·	·	5	·	·	·	·	·	·	·	13	·	·	·
BASS DRUM	1	·	·	·	5	·	·	·	9	·	·	·	13	·	·	·

NOTES

16 BEAT XI — 16 STEPS

INSTRUMENT	1	2	3	4	5	6	7	8	9	10	11	12	13	14	15	16
O. HI-HAT	·	·	3	·	·	·	7	·	·	·	·	·	·	·	·	·
C. HI-HAT	1	2	·	4	5	6	·	8	9	10	11	12	13	14	15	·
SNARE DRUM	·	·	·	·	5	·	·	·	·	10	·	·	13	·	·	16
TOM 3	·	·	·	·	5	·	·	·	·	·	·	·	13	·	·	·
BASS DRUM	1	·	·	·	5	·	·	·	9	·	·	·	13	·	·	·

NOTES

16 BEAT XII — 16 STEPS

INSTRUMENT	1	2	3	4	5	6	7	8	9	10	11	12	13	14	15	16
C. HI-HAT	1	2	·	4	5	·	7	8	·	10	·	12	·	·	·	·
SNARE DRUM	·	·	3	·	·	6	·	·	9	·	11	·	13	14	·	·
TOM 2	·	·	·	·	·	·	·	·	·	·	·	·	·	·	15	·
BASS DRUM	1	·	·	·	5	·	·	·	9	·	·	·	13	·	·	16
ACCENT	1	·	·	·	5	·	·	·	·	·	·	·	·	·	·	·

NOTES

16 BEAT XIII — 16 STEPS

INSTRUMENT	1	2	3	4	5	6	7	8	9	10	11	12	13	14	15	16
C. HI-HAT	·	2	3	·	5	6	·	8	·	10	·	12	·	14	·	·
SNARE DRUM	·	·	·	·	·	·	·	·	·	·	·	·	13	·	15	16
TOM 1	1	·	·	4	·	·	·	·	·	·	·	·	·	·	·	·
TOM 2	·	·	·	·	·	·	7	·	9	·	·	·	·	·	·	·
TOM 3	·	·	·	·	·	·	·	·	·	·	11	·	·	·	·	·
BASS DRUM	1	·	·	·	5	·	·	·	9	·	·	·	13	·	·	·

NOTES

16 BEAT XIV — 32 STEPS

INSTRUMENT	1	2	3	4	5	6	7	8	9	10	11	12	13	14	15	16	1	2	3	4	5	6	7	8	9	10	11	12	13	14	15	16
C. HI-HAT	1	2	3	4	5	·	7	·	9	·	11	·	13	·	15	·	1	·	3	·	5	·	7	·	9	·	11	·	13	·	15	·
SNARE DRUM	·	·	·	·	·	·	·	·	9	·	·	·	·	·	·	·	·	·	·	·	·	·	·	·	9	·	·	·	·	·	·	·
BASS DRUM	1	·	·	·	·	·	7	·	·	·	·	·	·	·	15	·	1	·	·	·	·	·	·	·	·	·	·	·	·	·	·	·
ACCENT	1	·	·	·	·	·	·	·	·	·	11	·	·	·	·	·	1	·	·	·	·	·	·	·	·	·	·	·	·	·	·	·

NOTES

16 BEAT XV   32 STEPS

INSTRUMENT	1	2	3	4	5	6	7	8	9	10	11	12	13	14	15	16	1	2	3	4	5	6	7	8	9	10	11	12	13	14	15	16
O. HI-HAT	·	·	·	·	·	·	·	·	·	·	·	·	·	·	15	·	·	2	·	·	·	·	·	·	9	·	·	·	·	·	·	·
C. HI-HAT	1	·	3	·	5	·	7	·	9	·	11	·	13	·	·	16	1	·	3	4	5	·	7	·	·	·	11	·	13	·	15	·
SNARE DRUM	·	·	·	·	·	·	·	·	9	·	·	·	·	·	·	·	·	·	·	·	·	·	·	·	9	·	·	·	·	·	·	·
BASS DRUM	1	·	·	·	5	·	·	·	9	·	·	·	13	·	·	·	1	·	·	·	5	·	·	·	9	·	·	·	13	·	·	·

NOTES

16 BEAT XVI   32 STEPS

INSTRUMENT	1	2	3	4	5	6	7	8	9	10	11	12	13	14	15	16	1	2	3	4	5	6	7	8	9	10	11	12	13	14	15	16
C. HI-HAT	·	·	3	·	·	·	·	·	·	·	11	·	·	·	15	·	·	·	3	·	5	·	·	·	·	·	·	·	·	·	·	·
SNARE DRUM	·	·	·	·	5	·	·	·	9	·	·	·	·	·	·	·	·	·	·	·	·	·	·	·	9	·	·	·	·	·	·	·
TOM 1	·	·	·	·	·	·	·	·	·	·	·	·	·	·	·	·	·	·	·	·	·	·	·	·	·	·	·	12	·	·	·	·
TOM 2	·	·	·	·	·	·	·	·	·	·	·	·	·	·	·	·	·	·	·	·	·	·	·	·	·	·	11	·	·	·	·	·
TOM 3	·	·	·	·	·	·	·	·	·	·	·	·	·	·	·	·	·	·	·	·	·	·	·	·	·	·	·	·	13	·	·	·
BASS DRUM	1	·	·	·	·	·	7	·	·	·	·	·	13	·	·	·	1	·	3	·	·	·	7	·	·	·	·	·	·	·	15	·

NOTES

16 BEAT XVII   32 STEPS

INSTRUMENT	1	2	3	4	5	6	7	8	9	10	11	12	13	14	15	16	1	2	3	4	5	6	7	8	9	10	11	12	13	14	15	16
SNARE DRUM	1	2	3	·	5	·	·	·	·	·	·	·	·	·	·	·	·	·	·	·	·	·	·	·	9	·	11	·	13	·	15	·
TOM 1	·	·	·	·	·	·	7	8	9	·	11	·	·	·	·	·	·	·	·	·	·	·	·	·	·	·	·	·	·	·	·	·
TOM 2	·	·	·	·	·	·	·	·	·	·	·	·	13	14	15	·	1	·	·	·	·	·	·	·	·	·	·	·	·	·	·	·
TOM 3	·	·	·	·	·	·	·	·	·	·	·	·	·	·	·	·	·	·	3	4	5	·	7	·	·	·	·	·	·	·	·	·
BASS DRUM	1	·	·	·	·	·	·	·	·	·	·	·	·	·	·	·	·	·	·	·	·	·	·	·	·	·	·	·	·	·	·	·

NOTES

16 BEAT XVIII   32 STEPS

INSTRUMENT	1	2	3	4	5	6	7	8	9	10	11	12	13	14	15	16	1	2	3	4	5	6	7	8	9	10	11	12	13	14	15	16
O. HI-HAT	·	·	·	·	·	·	7	·	·	·	11	·	·	·	·	·	·	·	·	·	·	·	·	·	·	·	·	·	·	·	·	·
C. HI-HAT	1	·	·	·	·	·	·	·	9	·	·	·	13	·	·	·	·	·	·	·	·	·	·	·	·	·	·	·	·	·	·	·
SNARE DRUM	1	·	3	·	5	·	7	·	·	·	11	·	·	·	·	·	·	·	·	·	·	·	·	·	·	·	·	·	·	·	·	·
TOM 1	·	·	·	·	·	·	·	·	·	·	·	·	·	·	15	16	1	·	3	·	·	·	·	·	·	·	·	·	·	·	·	·
TOM 2	·	·	·	·	·	·	·	·	·	·	·	·	·	·	·	·	·	·	·	·	5	·	7	·	·	·	·	·	·	·	·	·
TOM 3	·	·	·	·	·	·	·	·	·	·	·	·	·	·	·	·	·	·	·	·	·	·	·	·	9	·	11	·	13	·	·	·
BASS DRUM	1	·	·	·	·	·	·	·	9	·	·	·	·	·	·	·	1	·	·	·	·	·	·	·	9	·	·	·	·	·	15	·

NOTES

32 BEAT   32 STEPS

INSTRUMENT	1	2	3	4	5	6	7	8	9	10	11	12	13	14	15	16	1	2	3	4	5	6	7	8	9	10	11	12	13	14	15	16
O. HI-HAT	1	2	3	4	5	·	7	·	9	·	11	·	13	·	·	·	1	2	3	4	·	·	·	·	9	·	·	·	·	·	·	·
C. HI-HAT	·	·	·	·	·	·	·	·	·	·	·	·	·	·	15	·	·	·	·	·	5	·	·	·	·	·	·	·	13	·	·	·
SNARE DRUM	·	·	·	·	·	·	·	·	9	·	·	·	·	·	·	·	·	·	3	·	·	·	·	·	9	·	·	·	13	·	·	·
BASS DRUM	1	·	·	·	·	·	·	·	9	·	·	·	·	·	·	·	·	·	·	·	·	·	7	·	9	·	·	·	13	·	·	·
ACCENT	1	·	·	·	·	·	·	·	9	·	·	·	·	·	·	·	1	·	·	·	·	·	·	·	9	·	·	·	13	·	·	·
CYMBAL	·	·	·	·	·	·	·	·	·	·	·	·	·	·	·	·	·	·	·	·	·	·	·	·	·	·	·	·	·	·	·	·
HANDCLAP	·	·	·	·	·	·	·	·	·	·	·	·	·	·	·	·	·	·	·	·	·	·	·	·	·	·	·	·	·	·	·	·

NOTES

32 BEAT   32 STEPS

INSTRUMENT	1	2	3	4	5	6	7	8	9	10	11	12	13	14	15	16	1	2	3	4	5	6	7	8	9	10	11	12	13	14	15	16
COWBELL	1	·	·	4	·	6	7	·	·	·	·	12	·	14	15	·	1	·	·	4	·	6	7	·	·	·	·	12	·	14	15	·
C. HI-HAT	·	2	3	·	5	·	·	8	·	10	11	·	13	·	·	16	·	2	3	·	5	·	·	8	·	10	11	·	13	·	·	16
TOM	·	·	·	·	·	·	·	·	9	·	·	·	·	·	·	·	·	·	·	·	·	·	·	·	9	·	·	·	·	·	·	·
BASS DRUM	1	·	·	·	·	·	7	·	9	·	·	·	·	·	15	·	1	·	·	·	·	·	7	·	9	·	·	·	·	·	15	·

NOTES

32 BEAT   32 STEPS

INSTRUMENT	1	2	3	4	5	6	7	8	9	10	11	12	13	14	15	16	1	2	3	4	5	6	7	8	9	10	11	12	13	14	15	16
C. HI-HAT	1	2	3	·	5	·	·	8	·	10	11	·	13	·	·	16	1	2	3	·	5	·	·	8	·	10	11	12	13	·	15	16
SNARE DRUM	·	·	·	·	·	·	·	·	·	·	·	·	·	·	·	·	·	·	·	·	·	·	·	8	·	·	·	·	·	·	·	·
TOM 2	·	·	·	·	·	·	·	8	·	·	·	·	·	·	·	·	·	·	·	·	·	·	·	·	·	·	·	·	·	·	·	·
TOM 3	·	·	·	·	·	·	·	·	9	·	·	·	·	·	·	·	·	·	·	·	·	·	·	·	9	·	·	·	·	·	·	·
BASS DRUM	1	·	·	·	·	·	7	·	9	·	·	·	·	·	15	·	1	·	·	·	·	·	7	·	9	·	·	·	·	·	15	·
HANDCLAPS	1	·	·	4	·	6	7	·	·	·	·	12	·	14	15	·	1	·	·	4	·	6	7	·	·	10	11	12	13	·	15	·

NOTES

5/4 BEAT I   20 STEPS

INSTRUMENT	1	2	3	4	5	6	7	8	9	10	11	12	13	14	15	16	17	18	19	20
CYMBAL	1	·	·	·	5	·	·	8	9	·	·	·	13	·	·	·	17	·	·	·
SNARE DRUM	·	·	·	·	5	·	·	·	9	·	·	·	·	·	·	·	17	·	·	·
BASS DRUM	1	·	·	·	·	·	·	·	·	·	·	·	13	·	·	·	·	·	·	·

NOTES

5/4 BEAT II   20 STEPS

INSTRUMENT	1	2	3	4	5	6	7	8	9	10	11	12	13	14	15	16	17	18	19	20
CYMBAL	1	·	·	·	·	·	7	·	·	·	·	·	13	·	·	·	17	·	·	·
C. HI-HAT	1	·	3	·	5	·	7	·	9	·	11	·	13	·	15	·	17	·	19	·
RIM SHOT	1	·	·	·	·	·	7	·	·	·	·	·	13	·	·	·	17	·	·	·
HI-CONGA	·	·	·	·	5	·	7	·	·	·	·	·	·	·	15	·	17	18	19	20
LO-CONGA	·	·	3	·	·	·	·	·	9	·	·	·	·	·	·	·	·	·	·	·
BASS DRUM	1	·	·	·	·	·	7	·	·	·	·	·	13	·	·	·	17	·	·	·

NOTES

5/2 BEAT   20 STEPS

INSTRUMENT	1	2	3	4	5	6	7	8	9	10	11	12	13	14	15	16	17	18	19	20
O. HI-HAT	·	·	·	·	·	·	·	·	·	·	·	·	·	·	15	·	·	·	19	·
C. HI-HAT	1	·	3	·	5	·	7	·	9	·	11	·	13	14	15	16	17	18	19	20
SNARE DRUM	·	·	·	·	·	·	7	·	·	·	·	·	13	·	·	·	17	·	·	·
BASS DRUM	1	·	·	·	·	·	7	·	·	·	·	·	13	·	·	·	17	·	·	·

NOTES

12/8 VARIATION   12 STEPS

INSTRUMENT	1	2	3	4	5	6	7	8	9	10	11	12
C. HI-HAT	1	2	3	4	5	6	7	8	9	10	11	12
SNARE DRUM	·	·	·	4	·	·	·	·	·	·	11	·
BASS DRUM	1	2	·	·	·	6	7	·	9	·	·	·

NOTES

ROCK 1 16 STEPS

INSTRUMENT	1	2	3	4	5	6	7	8	9	10	11	12	13	14	15	16
C. HI-HAT	1	2	3	4	5	6	7	8	9	10	11	12	13	14	15	16
SNARE DRUM	·	·	3	·	·	·	7	·	·	·	11	·	·	·	15	·
BASS DRUM	1	·	·	4	5	·	·	8	9	·	·	12	13	·	·	16

NOTES

ROCK II 16 STEPS

INSTRUMENT	1	2	3	4	5	6	7	8	9	10	11	12	13	14	15	16
O. HI-HAT	·	2	·	4	·	6	·	8	·	10	·	12	·	14	·	16
C. HI-HAT	1	2	3	4	5	6	7	8	9	10	11	12	13	14	15	16
SNARE DRUM	·	·	3	·	·	·	7	·	·	·	11	·	·	·	15	·
BASS DRUM	1	·	3	·	5	6	·	8	9	·	11	·	13	14	·	16

NOTES

ROCK III 32 STEPS

INSTRUMENT	1	2	3	4	5	6	7	8	9	10	11	12	13	14	15	16	1	2	3	4	5	6	7	8	9	10	11	12	13	14	15	16
CYMBAL	1	·	3	4	5	·	7	·	9	·	11	·	13	·	15	·	1	·	3	4	5	·	7	·	9	·	11	·	13	·	15	·
SNARE DRUM	·	·	·	·	5	·	7	·	·	·	·	·	13	·	·	·	·	·	·	·	5	·	7	·	·	·	·	·	13	·	·	·
BASS DRUM	1	·	·	·	·	·	7	·	9	·	·	·	·	·	15	·	1	·	·	·	·	·	7	·	9	·	·	·	·	·	15	·

NOTES

ROCK IV 32 STEPS

INSTRUMENT	1	2	3	4	5	6	7	8	9	10	11	12	13	14	15	16	1	2	3	4	5	6	7	8	9	10	11	12	13	14	15	16
C. HI-HAT	1	·	3	·	5	·	7	·	9	·	11	·	13	·	15	·	1	·	3	·	5	·	7	·	9	·	11	·	13	·	15	·
SNARE DRUM	·	·	·	·	5	·	·	·	·	·	·	·	13	·	·	·	·	·	·	·	5	·	·	·	·	·	·	·	13	·	·	·
BASS DRUM	1	·	·	·	·	·	·	8	9	·	11	·	·	·	·	·	1	·	3	·	·	·	7	·	·	·	11	·	·	·	15	·

NOTES

ROCK V 32 STEPS

INSTRUMENT	1	2	3	4	5	6	7	8	9	10	11	12	13	14	15	16	1	2	3	4	5	6	7	8	9	10	11	12	13	14	15	16
O. HI-HAT	·	·	·	·	·	·	·	·	·	·	·	·	·	·	·	·	·	·	·	·	·	·	·	·	·	·	·	·	·	·	15	·
C. HI-HAT	1	·	3	·	5	·	7	·	9	·	11	·	13	·	15	·	1	·	3	·	5	·	7	·	9	·	11	·	13	·	15	·
SNARE DRUM	·	·	·	·	5	·	·	·	·	·	·	·	13	·	·	·	·	·	·	·	5	·	·	·	·	·	·	·	13	·	·	·
BASS DRUM	1	·	·	4	·	·	·	·	·	·	11	·	·	·	·	·	1	·	3	4	·	·	·	·	·	·	11	·	·	·	15	·

NOTES

ROCK VI 32 STEPS

INSTRUMENT	1	2	3	4	5	6	7	8	9	10	11	12	13	14	15	16	1	2	3	4	5	6	7	8	9	10	11	12	13	14	15	16
O. HI-HAT	·	·	·	·	·	·	·	·	·	·	·	·	·	·	·	·	·	·	·	·	·	·	·	·	·	·	11	·	·	·	15	·
C. HI-HAT	1	·	3	·	·	·	7	·	·	·	11	·	·	·	15	·	·	·	3	·	·	·	7	·	·	·	11	·	13	·	15	·
SNARE DRUM	·	·	·	·	5	·	·	·	·	·	·	·	13	·	·	·	·	·	·	·	5	·	·	·	·	·	·	·	13	·	·	·
BASS DRUM	1	·	·	·	·	·	7	·	9	·	·	12	·	·	15	·	1	·	·	·	·	·	7	·	9	·	11	·	·	·	15	·
COWBELL	1	·	·	·	5	·	·	·	9	·	·	·	13	·	·	·	1	·	·	·	5	·	·	·	9	·	·	·	13	·	·	·

NOTES

ROCK VII   32 STEPS

INSTRUMENT	1	2	3	4	5	6	7	8	9	10	11	12	13	14	15	16	1	2	3	4	5	6	7	8	9	10	11	12	13	14	15	16
O. HI-HAT	·	·	·	·	·	·	·	·	·	·	·	·	·	·	·	·	·	·	·	·	·	·	·	·	·	10	·	·	·	14	·	·
C. HI-HAT	1	2	3	4	5	6	7	8	9	10	11	12	13	14	15	16	1	2	3	4	5	6	7	8	9	10	·	12	13	14	·	16
SNARE DRUM	·	·	·	·	5	·	·	·	·	·	·	·	13	·	·	·	·	·	·	·	5	·	·	·	·	·	·	·	13	·	·	·
BASS DRUM	1	·	·	·	·	·	·	8	9	·	11	·	·	·	·	16	1	·	·	·	·	·	·	8	9	·	11	12	·	14	·	16

NOTES

ROCK VIII   32 STEPS

INSTRUMENT	1	2	3	4	5	6	7	8	9	10	11	12	13	14	15	16	1	2	3	4	5	6	7	8	9	10	11	12	13	14	15	16
C. HI-HAT	1	·	·	·	5	·	·	·	9	·	·	·	13	·	·	·	1	·	·	·	5	·	·	·	9	·	·	·	13	·	·	·
SNARE DRUM	·	·	·	·	5	·	·	·	·	·	·	·	13	·	·	·	·	·	·	·	5	·	·	·	·	·	·	·	13	·	·	·
BASS DRUM	1	·	4	5	·	·	·	9	·	·	12	·	14	·	·	1	·	4	5	·	·	·	9	·	·	12	·	14	·	16		
CYMBAL	·	·	3	·	·	·	7	·	·	·	11	·	·	·	15	·	·	·	3	·	·	·	7	·	·	·	11	·	·	·	15	·

NOTES

ROCK IX   32 STEPS

INSTRUMENT	1	2	3	4	5	6	7	8	9	10	11	12	13	14	15	16	1	2	3	4	5	6	7	8	9	10	11	12	13	14	15	16
O. HI-HAT	·	·	3	·	·	·	7	·	·	·	11	·	·	·	15	·	·	·	3	·	·	·	7	·	·	·	11	·	·	·	15	·
C. HI-HAT	1	2	3	4	5	6	7	8	9	10	11	12	13	14	15	16	1	2	3	4	5	6	7	8	9	10	11	12	13	14	15	16
SNARE DRUM	·	·	3	·	·	·	·	·	·	·	11	·	·	·	·	·	·	·	3	·	·	·	·	·	·	·	11	·	·	·	·	·
LOW CONGA	·	·	·	·	·	·	·	·	·	·	·	·	13	14	·	·	·	·	·	·	·	·	·	·	·	·	·	·	13	14	·	·
BASS DRUM	1	·	·	4	5	·	·	·	9	·	·	12	13	·	·	16	1	·	·	4	5	·	·	·	9	·	·	12	13	·	·	16
COWBELL	1	·	·	·	5	·	·	·	9	·	·	13	·	·	·		1	·	·	·	5	·	·	·	9	·	·	12	·	14	15	·

NOTES

ROCK X   16 STEPS

INSTRUMENT	1	2	3	4	5	6	7	8	9	10	11	12	13	14	15	16
O. HI-HAT	·	·	·	·	·	·	·	·	·	·	·	·	·	·	·	16
C. HI-HAT	1	·	·	·	·	·	·	·	·	·	·	·	·	·	·	16
SNARE DRUM	·	·	3	·	·	·	7	·	·	·	11	·	·	·	15	·
BASS DRUM	1	·	·	·	·	6	·	8	·	10	·	12	·	14	·	16
CYMBAL	1	·	3	·	5	·	7	·	9	·	11	·	13	·	15	·

NOTES

ROCK XI   16 STEPS

INSTRUMENT	1	2	3	4	5	6	7	8	9	10	11	12	13	14	15	16
O. HI-HAT	·	2	·	4	·	6	·	8	·	10	·	12	·	14	·	16
C. HI-HAT	1	2	3	4	5	6	7	8	9	10	11	12	13	14	15	16
SNARE DRUM	·	·	3	·	·	·	7	·	·	·	11	·	·	·	15	·
BASS DRUM	1	·	·	·	5	6	·	·	·	10	·	12	·	14	·	16

NOTES

ROCK XII   32 STEPS

INSTRUMENT	1	2	3	4	5	6	7	8	9	10	11	12	13	14	15	16	1	2	3	4	5	6	7	8	9	10	11	12	13	14	15	16
O. HI-HAT	·	·	·	·	·	·	·	·	·	·	·	·	·	·	·	·	·	·	·	·	·	·	·	·	·	10	·	·	·	14	·	·
C. HI-HAT	1	·	3	4	5	·	7	8	9	·	11	12	13	·	15	16	1	·	3	4	5	·	7	8	9	10	·	12	13	14	·	16
SNARE DRUM	·	·	·	·	5	·	·	·	·	·	·	·	13	·	·	·	·	·	·	·	5	·	·	·	·	·	·	·	13	·	·	·
BASS DRUM	1	·	·	·	·	·	·	·	9	·	11	·	·	·	·	·	1	·	·	·	·	·	·	·	9	·	11	·	·	·	15	·

NOTES

66

SLOW ROCK — 12 STEPS

INSTRUMENT	1	2	3	4	5	6	7	8	9	10	11	12
C. HI-HAT	1	2	3	4	5	6	7	8	9	10	11	12
O. HI-HAT	·	·	·	4	·	·	·	·	·	10	·	·
SNARE DRUM	·	·	·	4	·	·	·	·	·	10	·	·
BASS DRUM	1	·	·	·	·	6	7	·	·	·	·	12
ACCENT	·	·	·	·	·	·	·	·	·	·	·	·
CYMBAL	·	·	·	·	·	·	·	·	·	·	·	·
HANDCLAP	·	·	·	·	·	·	·	·	·	·	·	·

NOTES

FILL I — 16 STEPS

INSTRUMENT	1	2	3	4	5	6	7	8	9	10	11	12	13	14	15	16
C. HI-HAT	·	·	·	·	·	·	·	·	·	·	·	·	·	·	·	·
O. HI-HAT	·	·	·	·	·	·	·	·	·	·	·	·	·	·	·	·
SNARE DRUM	1	·	·	4	5	·	·	8	9	·	·	·	·	·	·	·
BASS DRUM	·	2	·	·	·	6	·	·	·	10	·	12	·	14	·	16
ACCENT	1	2	·	·	5	6	·	·	9	10	·	12	·	14	·	16
CYMBAL	·	·	·	·	·	·	·	·	·	·	·	·	·	·	·	·
HANDCLAP	·	·	·	·	·	·	·	·	·	·	·	·	·	·	·	·

NOTES

AFRO ROCK — 12 STEPS

INSTRUMENT	1	2	3	4	5	6	7	8	9	10	11	12
O. HI-HAT	1	·	3	·	5	·	7	·	9	·	11	·
SNARE DRUM	·	·	·	4	5	·	·	·	·	10	·	·
TOM 1	·	·	·	·	·	·	7	8	9	·	·	·
TOM 2	1	·	3	·	·	6	·	·	·	10	11	·
TOM 3	·	·	·	·	·	·	·	·	·	·	·	12
BASS DRUM	1	·	·	4	·	·	·	·	·	10	·	·
ACCENT	·	·	·	4	·	6	·	·	·	10	·	·

NOTES

FILL II — 16 STEPS

INSTRUMENT	1	2	3	4	5	6	7	8	9	10	11	12	13	14	15	16
C. HI-HAT	·	·	·	·	·	·	·	·	·	·	·	·	·	·	·	·
O. HI-HAT	·	·	·	·	·	·	·	·	·	·	·	·	·	·	·	·
SNARE DRUM	·	2	3	4	·	6	7	8	·	10	11	12	13	14	15	·
BASS DRUM	1	·	·	·	5	·	·	·	9	·	·	·	13	·	·	·
ACCENT	1	·	·	4	5	·	·	8	9	·	·	12	13	14	15	·
CYMBAL	1	·	·	·	·	·	·	·	·	·	·	·	13	·	·	·
HANDCLAP	·	·	·	·	·	·	·	·	·	·	·	·	·	·	·	·

NOTES

SLOW BLUES — 12 STEPS

INSTRUMENT	1	2	3	4	5	6	7	8	9	10	11	12
C. HI-HAT	1	·	·	4	·	·	7	·	·	10	·	·
SNARE DRUM	·	·	·	4	·	·	·	·	·	10	·	·
BASS DRUM	1	·	·	·	·	6	7	·	·	·	·	·
C. HI-HAT	1	·	·	4	·	·	7	·	·	10	·	·

NOTES

FILL III — 16 STEPS

INSTRUMENT	1	2	3	4	5	6	7	8	9	10	11	12	13	14	15	16
TOM 1	1	2	3	·	·	·	·	·	·	·	·	·	·	·	·	·
TOM 2	·	·	·	4	5	6	·	·	·	·	·	·	·	·	·	·
TOM 3	·	·	·	·	·	·	7	8	9	·	11	·	13	·	15	·
BASS DRUM	1	·	·	·	5	·	·	·	9	·	·	·	13	·	·	·

NOTES

BOOGIE WOOGIE — 12 STEPS

INSTRUMENT	1	2	3	4	5	6	7	8	9	10	11	12
C. HI-HAT	1	·	·	·	·	·	7	·	·	·	·	·
O. HI-HAT	·	·	·	4	·	·	·	·	·	10	·	·
SNARE DRUM	·	·	·	4	·	·	·	·	·	10	·	·
BASS DRUM	1	·	·	·	·	·	7	·	9	·	·	·
ACCENT	1	·	·	4	·	·	7	·	·	10	·	·
CYMBAL	1	·	·	4	·	·	7	·	·	10	·	·
HANDCLAP	·	·	·	·	·	·	·	·	·	·	·	·

NOTES

FILL IV — 32 STEPS

INSTRUMENT	1	2	3	4	5	6	7	8	9	10	11	12	13	14	15	16	1	2	3	4	5	6	7	8	9	10	11	12	13	14	15	16
SNARE DRUM	1	·	3	4	5	·	7	·	·	·	·	·	·	·	·	·	·	·	·	·	·	·	·	·	·	·	·	·	·	·	·	·
TOM 1	·	·	·	·	·	·	·	·	9	·	11	·	13	·	15	·	·	·	·	·	·	·	·	·	·	·	·	·	·	·	·	·
TOM 2	·	·	·	·	·	·	·	·	·	·	·	·	·	·	·	·	1	·	3	·	5	·	7	·	·	·	·	·	·	·	·	·
TOM 3	·	·	·	·	·	·	·	·	·	·	·	·	·	·	·	·	·	·	·	·	·	·	·	·	9	·	11	·	13	·	15	·
BASS DRUM	1	·	·	·	·	·	·	·	9	·	·	·	·	·	·	·	1	·	·	·	·	·	·	·	9	·	·	·	·	·	·	·
ACCENT	1	·	·	·	5	·	7	·	9	·	11	·	13	·	15	·	1	·	3	·	5	·	7	·	9	·	11	·	13	·	15	·

NOTES

FILL V — 32 STEPS

INSTRUMENT	1	2	3	4	5	6	7	8	9	10	11	12	13	14	15	16	1	2	3	4	5	6	7	8	9	10	11	12	13	14	15	16
SNARE DRUM	·	·	·	·	·	·	·	·	·	·	11	12	13	·	·	·	·	·	·	·	·	·	·	·	·	·	·	·	·	·	·	·
TOM 1	·	·	·	·	·	·	·	·	·	·	·	·	·	·	·	·	1	·	3	·	·	·	7	·	·	·	·	·	·	·	·	·
TOM 2	·	·	·	·	·	·	·	·	·	·	·	·	·	·	·	·	·	·	·	·	·	·	·	·	·	·	11	·	·	·	·	·
TOM 3	·	·	·	·	·	·	·	·	·	·	·	·	·	·	·	·	·	·	·	·	·	·	·	·	·	·	·	·	13	·	·	·
BASS DRUM	1	·	·	·	·	·	·	·	9	·	·	·	·	·	15	·	1	·	·	·	5	·	·	·	9	·	·	·	·	·	·	·
ACCENT	·	·	·	·	·	·	·	·	·	·	·	·	13	·	·	·	1	·	3	·	·	·	7	·	·	·	11	·	13	·	·	·

NOTES

POPS I — 16 STEPS

INSTRUMENT	1	2	3	4	5	6	7	8	9	10	11	12	13	14	15	16
C. HI-HAT	1	2	3	4	5	6	7	8	9	10	11	12	13	14	15	16
RIM SHOT	·	·	3	·	·	·	7	·	·	·	11	·	·	·	15	·
BASS DRUM	1	·	·	4	5	·	·	8	9	·	·	12	13	·	·	16

NOTES

POPS II — 32 STEPS

INSTRUMENT	1	2	3	4	5	6	7	8	9	10	11	12	13	14	15	16	1	2	3	4	5	6	7	8	9	10	11	12	13	14	15	16
O. HI-HAT	·	·	·	·	·	·	·	·	·	·	·	·	·	·	·	·	·	·	·	·	·	·	·	·	·	·	·	·	·	·	15	·
C. HI-HAT	1	·	3	4	5	·	7	8	9	·	11	12	13	·	15	16	1	·	3	4	5	·	7	8	9	·	11	12	13	14	15	·
SNARE DRUM	·	·	·	·	5	·	·	·	·	·	·	·	13	·	·	·	·	·	·	·	5	·	·	·	·	·	·	·	13	·	·	·
BASS DRUM	1	·	·	·	·	·	7	·	9	·	·	·	·	·	·	·	1	·	3	·	·	·	7	·	9	·	·	·	·	·	15	·

NOTES

POPS III — 16 STEPS

INSTRUMENT	1	2	3	4	5	6	7	8	9	10	11	12	13	14	15	16
CYMBAL	1	2	3	4	5	6	7	8	9	10	11	12	13	14	15	16
RIM SHOT	·	·	3	·	·	·	7	·	·	·	11	·	·	·	15	·
BASS DRUM	1	·	·	4	5	·	·	·	9	10	·	12	13	·	·	16

NOTES

ELECTRO-POP I — 16 STEPS

INSTRUMENT	1	2	3	4	5	6	7	8	9	10	11	12	13	14	15	16
C. HI-HAT	1	·	3	4	5	·	7	8	9	·	11	12	13	·	15	16
O. HI-HAT	·	·	·	·	·	·	·	·	·	·	·	·	·	·	·	·
SNARE DRUM	·	·	·	·	5	·	·	·	·	·	·	·	13	·	·	·
BASS DRUM	1	·	·	·	5	·	·	·	9	·	·	·	13	·	·	·
ACCENT	1	·	·	·	5	·	·	·	9	·	·	·	13	·	·	·
CYMBAL	1	·	·	·	·	·	·	·	·	·	·	·	·	·	·	·
HANDCLAP	·	·	·	·	5	·	·	·	·	·	·	·	13	·	·	·

NOTES

NEW WAVE I — 16 STEPS

INSTRUMENT	1	2	3	4	5	6	7	8	9	10	11	12	13	14	15	16
O. HI-HAT	·	·	·	·	·	·	·	·	·	·	·	·	13	·	·	·
C. HI-HAT	1	·	·	·	5	·	·	·	9	·	·	·	·	·	15	·
SNARE DRUM	·	·	·	·	·	·	7	·	·	·	·	·	·	·	15	·
BASS DRUM	1	·	·	·	5	·	·	·	·	10	·	·	13	·	·	16
HANDCLAPS	·	2	3	4	·	·	7	·	·	10	11	12	·	·	·	·
ACCENT	1	·	3	·	·	·	7	·	·	10	11	12	13	·	·	·

NOTES

ELECTRO-POP II — 16 STEPS

INSTRUMENT	1	2	3	4	5	6	7	8	9	10	11	12	13	14	15	16
C. HI-HAT	1	·	3	4	5	·	7	·	·	·	·	·	·	·	15	16
O. HI-HAT	·	·	·	·	·	·	·	8	·	10	·	·	13	·	·	·
SNARE DRUM	·	·	·	·	5	·	·	·	·	·	·	·	13	·	·	·
BASS DRUM	1	·	·	4	·	·	·	8	·	·	·	12	·	·	15	·
ACCENT	1	·	·	·	5	·	·	·	9	·	·	·	13	·	15	·
CYMBAL	1	·	·	·	·	·	·	·	·	·	·	·	·	·	·	·
HANDCLAP	·	·	·	·	·	·	·	·	·	·	·	·	·	·	15	·

NOTES

NEW WAVE II — 16 STEPS

INSTRUMENT	1	2	3	4	5	6	7	8	9	10	11	12	13	14	15	16
C. HI-HAT	1	2	·	·	5	6	·	·	9	10	·	·	·	·	15	16
TOM 1	·	·	·	·	·	·	·	·	·	·	·	·	13	14	·	·
TOM 2	1	·	·	·	·	·	·	·	·	·	·	·	·	·	15	16
BASS DRUM	·	·	·	4	·	·	7	8	·	·	11	12	13	·	·	·
HANDCLAPS	1	2	3	4	·	·	·	·	·	·	·	·	·	·	15	·

NOTES

COMPU POP — 32 STEPS

INSTRUMENT	1	2	3	4	5	6	7	8	9	10	11	12	13	14	15	16	1	2	3	4	5	6	7	8	9	10	11	12	13	14	15	16
O. HI-HAT	·	·	·	·	·	·	·	·	·	·	·	·	·	·	·	·	·	·	·	·	·	·	·	·	·	·	·	·	·	·	15	·
C. HI-HAT	1	·	3	·	5	·	7	·	9	·	11	·	13	·	15	·	1	·	3	·	5	·	7	·	9	·	11	·	13	·	·	·
SNARE DRUM	·	·	·	·	5	·	·	·	·	·	·	·	13	·	·	·	·	·	·	·	5	·	·	·	·	·	·	·	13	·	·	·
BASS DRUM	·	·	·	·	5	·	·	·	9	·	·	·	13	·	·	·	·	·	3	·	·	·	·	·	·	·	·	·	·	·	15	·
CABASA	1	·	3	·	·	·	7	·	·	·	11	·	·	·	15	·	1	·	3	·	·	·	7	·	·	·	11	·	·	·	15	·
HI CONGA	·	·	3	·	·	·	·	·	·	·	·	·	·	·	15	·	·	·	·	·	·	·	·	·	·	·	·	·	·	13	·	15 ·
LO CONGA	·	·	·	·	5	·	·	·	9	·	·	·	13	·	·	·	·	·	·	·	·	·	·	·	·	·	·	·	·	13	·	15 ·

NOTES

69

DISCO I — 16 STEPS

INSTRUMENT	1	2	3	4	5	6	7	8	9	10	11	12	13	14	15	16
C. HI-HAT	1	·	·	·	5	·	·	·	9	·	·	·	13	·	·	·
O. HI-HAT	·	·	3	·	·	·	7	·	·	·	11	·	·	·	15	·
SNARE DRUM	·	·	·	·	5	·	·	·	·	·	·	·	13	·	·	·
BASS DRUM	1	·	·	·	5	·	·	·	9	·	·	·	13	·	·	·
ACCENT	1	·	·	·	5	·	·	·	9	·	·	·	13	·	·	·
CYMBAL	1	·	·	·	·	·	·	·	·	·	·	·	·	·	·	·
HANDCLAP	·	·	·	·	5	·	·	·	·	·	·	·	13	·	·	·

NOTES

DISCO II — 16 STEPS

INSTRUMENT	1	2	3	4	5	6	7	8	9	10	11	12	13	14	15	16
C. HI-HAT	1	2	3	4	5	6	7	8	9	10	11	12	13	14	15	16
SNARE DRUM	·	·	3	·	·	·	7	·	·	·	11	·	·	·	15	·
BASS DRUM	1	·	3	·	5	·	7	·	9	·	11	·	13	·	15	·

NOTES

DISCO III — 32 STEPS

INSTRUMENT	1	2	3	4	5	6	7	8	9	10	11	12	13	14	15	16	1	2	3	4	5	6	7	8	9	10	11	12	13	14	15	16
O. HI-HAT	·	·	3	·	·	·	7	·	·	·	11	·	·	·	15	·	·	·	3	·	·	·	7	·	·	·	11	·	·	·	15	·
C. HI-HAT	1	2	3	·	5	6	7	·	9	10	11	·	13	14	15	·	1	·	·	·	·	·	·	·	·	·	·	·	·	·	·	·
SNARE DRUM	·	·	·	·	5	·	·	·	·	·	·	·	13	·	·	·	·	·	·	·	5	·	·	·	·	·	·	·	13	·	·	·
BASS DRUM	1	·	·	·	5	·	·	·	9	·	·	·	13	·	·	·	1	·	·	·	5	·	·	·	9	·	·	·	13	·	·	·

NOTES

DISCO IV — 32 STEPS

INSTRUMENT	1	2	3	4	5	6	7	8	9	10	11	12	13	14	15	16	1	2	3	4	5	6	7	8	9	10	11	12	13	14	15	16
O. HI-HAT	·	·	·	·	·	·	·	·	·	·	·	·	·	·	15	·	·	·	·	·	·	·	·	·	·	·	·	·	·	·	15	·
C. HI-HAT	1	2	3	4	5	6	7	8	9	10	11	12	13	14	15	·	1	2	3	4	5	6	7	8	9	10	11	12	13	14	15	·
SNARE DRUM	·	·	·	·	5	·	·	·	·	·	·	·	13	·	·	·	·	·	·	·	5	·	·	·	·	·	·	·	13	·	·	·
BASS DRUM	1	·	·	·	5	·	·	·	9	·	·	·	13	·	·	·	1	·	·	·	5	·	·	·	9	·	·	·	13	·	·	·

NOTES

DISCO V — 32 STEPS

INSTRUMENT	1	2	3	4	5	6	7	8	9	10	11	12	13	14	15	16	1	2	3	4	5	6	7	8	9	10	11	12	13	14	15	16
O. HI-HAT	·	·	·	·	·	·	·	·	·	·	·	·	·	·	·	·	·	·	·	·	·	·	·	·	·	10	·	·	·	14	·	·
C. HI-HAT	1	2	3	4	5	6	7	8	9	10	11	12	13	14	15	16	1	2	3	4	5	6	7	8	9	10	·	12	13	14	·	16
SNARE DRUM	·	·	·	·	5	·	·	·	·	·	·	·	13	·	·	·	·	·	·	·	5	·	·	·	·	·	·	·	13	·	·	·
BASS DRUM	1	·	·	4	·	·	7	·	·	·	11	·	·	·	15	·	1	·	·	4	·	·	7	·	9	10	·	·	13	14	·	·

NOTES

DISCO VI — 32 STEPS

INSTRUMENT	1	2	3	4	5	6	7	8	9	10	11	12	13	14	15	16	1	2	3	4	5	6	7	8	9	10	11	12	13	14	15	16
O. HI-HAT	·	·	·	·	·	·	·	·	·	·	·	·	·	·	·	·	·	·	·	·	·	·	·	·	·	10	·	·	·	14	·	·
C. HI-HAT	1	·	3	4	5	·	7	8	9	·	11	12	13	·	15	16	1	·	3	4	5	·	7	8	9	10	·	12	13	14	·	16
SNARE DRUM	·	·	·	·	5	·	·	·	·	·	·	·	13	·	·	·	·	·	·	·	5	·	·	·	·	·	·	·	13	·	·	·
BASS DRUM	1	·	·	4	·	·	·	·	9	·	11	12	·	·	·	16	1	·	·	4	·	·	·	·	9	·	11	12	·	14	·	16

NOTES

DISCO VII — 32 STEPS

INSTRUMENT	1	2	3	4	5	6	7	8	9	10	11	12	13	14	15	16	1	2	3	4	5	6	7	8	9	10	11	12	13	14	15	16
O. HI-HAT	·	·	3	·	·	·	7	·	·	·	11	·	·	·	15	·	·	·	3	·	·	·	7	·	·	·	11	·	·	·	15	·
C. HI-HAT	1	2	3	·	5	6	7	·	9	10	11	·	13	14	15	·	1	2	3	·	5	6	7	·	9	10	11	·	13	14	15	·
SNARE DRUM	·	·	·	·	5	·	·	·	·	·	·	·	13	·	·	·	·	·	·	·	5	·	·	·	·	·	·	·	13	·	·	·
LO TOM	·	·	·	·	·	·	·	·	·	·	·	·	·	14	·	·	·	·	·	·	·	·	·	·	·	·	·	·	·	14	·	·
BASS DRUM	1	·	·	·	5	·	·	·	9	·	·	·	13	·	·	·	1	·	·	·	5	·	·	·	9	·	·	·	13	·	·	·
COWBELL	1	·	·	·	5	·	·	·	9	·	·	·	13	·	·	·	1	·	·	·	5	·	·	·	9	·	·	·	13	·	·	16

NOTES

DISCO VIII — 32 STEPS

INSTRUMENT	1	2	3	4	5	6	7	8	9	10	11	12	13	14	15	16	1	2	3	4	5	6	7	8	9	10	11	12	13	14	15	16
ACCENT	·	·	·	·	·	·	·	·	·	·	·	·	·	·	15	·	·	·	·	·	·	·	·	·	·	·	·	·	·	·	15	·
O. HI-HAT	·	·	·	·	·	·	·	·	·	·	·	·	·	·	·	·	·	·	·	·	·	·	·	·	·	·	·	·	·	·	·	·
C. HI-HAT	1	·	3	·	5	·	7	·	9	·	11	·	13	·	15	·	1	·	3	·	5	·	7	·	9	·	11	·	13	·	15	·
SNARE DRUM	·	·	·	·	5	·	·	·	·	·	·	·	·	·	15	·	·	·	·	·	5	·	·	·	·	·	11	·	13	·	15	·
HANDCLAPS	·	·	·	·	·	·	·	·	·	·	·	·	·	·	15	·	·	·	·	·	·	·	·	·	·	·	11	·	13	·	15	·
HI-TOM	·	·	·	·	·	·	·	·	9	·	11	·	·	·	15	·	·	·	·	·	5	6	·	·	9	·	11	·	·	·	15	·
LOW-TOM	·	·	·	·	·	·	7	·	·	·	·	·	13	·	·	·	·	·	3	·	·	·	7	·	·	·	·	·	13	·	15	·
BASS DRUM	1	·	·	·	·	·	7	·	9	·	·	·	·	·	15	·	·	·	·	·	·	·	7	·	9	·	·	·	·	·	15	·

NOTES

DISCO IX — 16 STEPS

INSTRUMENT	1	2	3	4	5	6	7	8	9	10	11	12	13	14	15	16
O. HI-HAT	·	·	3	·	·	·	7	·	·	·	11	·	·	·	15	·
C. HI-HAT	1	·	·	·	5	·	·	·	9	·	·	·	13	·	·	·
SNARE DRUM	·	·	·	·	5	·	·	·	·	·	·	·	13	·	·	·
BASS DRUM	1	·	·	4	5	·	·	·	9	·	·	·	13	·	·	·
HANDCLAPS	·	·	·	·	·	·	·	·	·	·	·	·	13	·	15	·
ACCENT	1	·	·	·	5	·	·	·	9	·	·	·	13	·	·	·

NOTES

REGGAE I — 12 STEPS

INSTRUMENT	1	2	3	4	5	6	7	8	9	10	11	12
C. HI-HAT	1	·	·	4	·	6	7	·	·	10	·	12
O. HI-HAT	·	·	·	·	·	·	·	·	·	·	·	·
SNARE DRUM	·	·	·	·	·	·	7	·	·	·	·	·
BASS DRUM	·	·	·	·	·	·	7	·	·	·	·	·
ACCENT	·	·	·	4	·	·	7	·	·	10	·	·
CYMBAL	·	·	·	·	·	·	·	·	·	·	·	·
HANDCLAP	·	·	·	·	·	·	·	·	·	·	·	·

NOTES

REGGAE II — 12 STEPS

INSTRUMENT	1	2	3	4	5	6	7	8	9	10	11	12
C. HI-HAT	·	2	·	4	·	6	7	·	·	10	·	12
SNARE DRUM	·	2	·	4	·	6	·	·	·	10	·	12
TOM	·	·	·	·	·	·	7	·	9	·	·	·
BASS DRUM	1	·	·	·	·	6	·	·	·	·	·	·
ACCENT	·	·	·	·	·	·	7	·	·	·	·	·

NOTES

REGGAE III — 12 STEPS

INSTRUMENT	1	2	3	4	5	6	7	8	9	10	11	12
C. HI-HAT	1	·	·	4	·	6	7	·	·	10	·	12
SNARE DRUM	·	·	·	·	·	·	7	·	·	·	·	·
BASS DRUM	·	·	·	·	·	·	7	·	·	·	·	·
ACCENT	·	·	·	·	·	·	7	·	·	·	·	·

NOTES

REGGAE IV — 24 STEPS

INSTRUMENT	1	2	3	4	5	6	7	8	9	10	11	12	1	2	3	4	5	6	7	8	9	10	11	12
O. HI-HAT	·	·	·	4	·	·	·	·	·	10	·	·	·	·	·	4	·	·	·	·	·	10	·	·
C. HI-HAT	1	·	3	·	·	·	7	·	9	·	·	·	1	·	3	·	·	·	7	·	9	·	·	·
RIM SHOT	1	·	·	·	·	·	7	·	·	·	·	·	1	·	·	·	·	·	7	·	·	·	·	·
BASS DRUM	·	·	·	·	·	·	7	·	·	10	·	·	·	·	3	·	·	·	7	·	·	·	·	·

NOTES

REGGAE DISCO — 32 STEPS

INSTRUMENT	1	2	3	4	5	6	7	8	9	10	11	12	13	14	15	16	1	2	3	4	5	6	7	8	9	10	11	12	13	14	15	16
O. HI-HAT	·	·	·	·	·	·	·	·	·	·	·	·	·	·	·	·	·	·	·	·	·	·	·	·	·	·	·	·	·	·	15	·
C. HI-HAT	1	·	3	4	5	·	7	8	9	·	11	12	13	·	15	16	1	·	3	4	5	·	7	8	9	·	11	12	13	·	·	·
SNARE	·	·	·	·	·	·	7	·	·	·	·	·	13	·	·	·	·	·	·	·	·	·	7	·	·	·	·	·	13	·	·	·
HANDCLAP	·	·	·	·	·	·	·	·	·	·	·	·	·	·	·	·	·	·	·	·	·	·	·	·	·	·	·	·	·	·	15	·
BASS	1	·	·	4	·	·	·	·	·	·	11	·	·	·	·	·	1	·	·	4	·	·	7	·	·	·	11	·	·	·	·	·
CABASA	1	2	·	4	5	6	·	8	9	10	·	12	13	14	·	16	1	2	·	4	5	6	·	8	9	10	·	12	13	14	·	16
WOOD BLOCK	1	2	·	·	·	·	7	8	·	·	·	·	·	·	·	·	1	2	·	·	·	·	7	8	·	·	·	·	·	·	·	·
COWBELL	1	·	·	4	·	·	7	·	9	·	·	12	·	·	15	·	1	·	·	4	·	·	7	·	9	·	·	12	·	·	15	·
HI AGOGO	·	·	·	·	·	·	·	·	·	·	·	·	·	·	·	·	·	·	·	·	·	·	·	·	·	·	·	12	13	·	·	·
LO AGOGO	·	·	·	·	·	·	·	·	·	·	·	·	·	·	·	·	·	·	·	·	·	·	·	·	·	10	·	·	·	·	·	·

NOTES

TECHNO SOUL — 32 STEPS

INSTRUMENT	1	2	3	4	5	6	7	8	9	10	11	12	13	14	15	16	1	2	3	4	5	6	7	8	9	10	11	12	13	14	15	16
C. HI-HAT	1	2	3	4	5	6	7	8	9	10	11	12	13	14	15	16	1	2	3	4	5	6	7	8	9	10	11	12	13	14	15	16
SNARE DRUM	·	·	·	·	5	·	·	·	·	·	·	·	13	·	·	·	·	·	·	·	5	·	·	·	·	·	·	·	13	·	·	·
BASS DRUM	·	2	3	·	5	·	7	·	9	10	·	12	·	·	15	16	·	2	3	·	5	·	7	·	9	10	·	12	·	14	15	·
HANDCLAPS	·	·	·	·	5	·	·	·	·	·	·	·	13	·	·	·	·	·	·	·	5	·	·	·	·	10	·	·	13	·	·	·
CABASA	1	2	3	4	5	·	·	·	·	·	·	·	·	·	·	·	1	2	3	4	5	·	·	·	·	·	·	·	·	·	·	·

NOTES

LATIN SOUL — 32 STEPS

INSTRUMENT	1	2	3	4	5	6	7	8	9	10	11	12	13	14	15	16	1	2	3	4	5	6	7	8	9	10	11	12	13	14	15	16
ACCENT	1	·	·	·	5	·	·	·	9	·	·	·	13	·	·	·	1	·	·	·	5	·	·	·	9	·	·	·	13	·	·	·
O. HI-HAT	·	·	·	·	·	·	·	·	·	·	·	·	·	·	·	·	·	·	·	·	·	·	·	·	·	·	·	·	·	·	15	·
C. HI-HAT	1	·	3	·	5	·	7	·	9	·	11	·	13	·	15	·	1	·	3	·	5	·	7	·	9	·	11	·	13	·	·	·
SNARE DRUM	·	·	·	·	5	·	·	·	·	·	·	·	13	·	·	·	·	·	·	·	5	·	·	·	·	·	·	·	13	·	·	·
HANDCLAPS	·	·	·	·	5	·	·	·	·	·	·	·	13	·	·	·	·	·	·	·	5	·	·	·	·	10	·	·	13	·	·	·
BASS DRUM	1	·	·	4	·	·	·	8	9	·	·	·	·	·	15	·	1	·	·	4	·	·	·	8	9	·	·	·	·	·	15	·
ACCENT (P)	·	·	3	·	·	·	7	·	·	·	11	·	·	·	15	·	·	·	3	·	·	·	7	·	·	·	11	·	·	·	15	·
CABASA	1	2	3	4	5	6	7	8	9	10	11	12	13	14	15	16	1	2	3	4	5	6	7	8	9	10	11	12	13	14	15	16
WOOD BLOCK	·	·	·	·	·	·	7	·	·	·	·	·	·	·	15	·	·	·	·	·	·	·	7	·	·	10	·	12	13	·	15	·
COW BELL	·	·	·	·	5	·	·	8	·	·	·	·	·	·	·	·	·	·	3	·	5	·	7	8	·	10	·	12	13	·	·	·
HI AGOGO	·	·	·	·	·	·	7	·	·	·	·	·	·	·	15	·	·	·	·	·	·	·	7	·	·	·	·	·	·	·	15	·
LO AGOGO	1	·	·	4	·	·	·	·	9	·	·	12	·	·	·	·	1	·	·	4	·	·	·	·	9	·	·	12	·	·	·	·

NOTES

AOR SAMBA — 32 STEPS

INSTRUMENT	1	2	3	4	5	6	7	8	9	10	11	12	13	14	15	16	1	2	3	4	5	6	7	8	9	10	11	12	13	14	15	16
O. HI-HAT	1	·	·	·	5	·	·	·	9	·	·	·	13	·	·	·	1	·	·	·	5	·	·	·	9	·	·	·	13	·	·	·
C. HI-HAT	·	·	3	4	·	·	7	8	·	·	11	12	·	·	15	16	·	·	3	4	·	·	7	8	·	·	11	12	·	·	15	16
SNARE DRUM	·	·	·	4	·	·	·	·	·	·	·	·	·	·	·	·	·	·	·	4	·	·	·	·	·	·	·	·	·	·	·	·
BASS DRUM	1	·	·	4	5	·	·	8	9	·	·	12	13	·	·	16	1	·	·	4	5	·	·	8	9	·	·	12	13	14	·	16
CABASA	1	2	·	4	5	6	·	8	9	10	·	12	13	14	·	16	1	2	·	4	5	6	·	8	9	10	·	12	13	14	·	16
HI AGOGO	·	·	·	·	·	6	·	·	·	10	·	·	·	·	·	·	·	·	·	·	·	6	·	·	·	10	·	·	·	·	·	·
LO AGOGO	·	·	·	4	·	·	7	·	·	·	·	·	·	·	·	·	·	·	·	4	·	·	7	·	·	·	·	·	·	·	·	·
HI CONGA	·	·	·	4	5	·	·	·	·	·	·	12	13	·	·	16	·	·	·	4	5	·	·	·	·	·	·	12	13	·	·	·
LO CONGA	1	·	·	·	·	·	7	·	9	·	·	·	·	14	·	·	·	·	·	·	·	·	7	·	9	·	·	·	·	14	·	·

NOTES

SALSA 32 STEPS

INSTRUMENT	1	2	3	4	5	6	7	8	9	10	11	12	13	14	15	16	1	2	3	4	5	6	7	8	9	10	11	12	13	14	15	16
O. HI-HAT	·	·	·	·	·	·	·	·	·	·	·	·	·	·	·	·	·	·	·	·	·	·	·	·	·	·	·	·	·	·	15	·
C. HI-HAT	1	·	3	4	5	6	7	8	9	10	11	12	13	14	15	16	1	·	3	4	5	6	7	8	9	10	11	12	13	14	·	·
SNARE DRUM	·	·	·	4	·	·	·	·	·	·	·	·	13	·	·	·	·	·	3	·	·	·	·	·	·	·	·	·	13	·	·	·
BASS DRUM	1	·	·	·	·	·	·	8	·	·	11	·	·	14	·	·	·	·	·	·	·	6	·	8	·	·	·	12	·	·	15	·
TIMBALES	·	·	·	·	·	·	·	·	·	·	·	·	·	·	·	·	·	·	·	·	·	·	·	·	·	10	11	12	13	·	15	16
HI CONGA	·	·	3	·	·	6	·	·	·	10	·	·	13	·	15	16	·	·	3	·	·	6	7	8	·	10	11	12	13	·	15	16
LO CONGA	1	·	·	·	·	7	8	9	·	·	12	·	·	·	·	·	·	·	·	·	·	·	·	·	9	·	·	·	·	14	·	·

NOTES

LATIN PROGRESSIVE 32 STEPS

INSTRUMENT	1	2	3	4	5	6	7	8	9	10	11	12	13	14	15	16	1	2	3	4	5	6	7	8	9	10	11	12	13	14	15	16
O. HI-HAT	1	·	·	·	·	·	·	·	·	·	·	·	·	·	·	·	·	·	·	·	·	·	·	·	·	·	·	·	·	·	·	·
C. HI-HAT	·	·	·	·	5	·	7	·	9	·	11	·	13	·	15	·	1	·	3	·	5	·	7	·	9	·	11	·	13	·	15	·
SNARE DRUM	·	·	·	·	5	·	·	·	·	·	·	·	13	·	·	·	·	·	·	·	5	·	·	·	·	·	·	·	13	·	·	·
BASS DRUM	1	·	·	·	·	·	7	·	9	·	·	·	·	·	15	·	·	·	·	·	·	·	7	·	9	·	·	·	·	·	·	·
TIMBALES	·	·	·	·	5	·	·	·	·	·	·	·	13	·	·	·	·	·	·	·	5	·	·	·	·	·	·	·	13	·	·	·
COWBELL	·	·	·	·	5	·	·	·	9	·	·	·	13	·	·	·	1	·	·	·	5	·	·	·	9	·	·	·	13	·	·	·
HI CONGA	·	·	·	·	5	·	·	·	·	·	·	·	13	·	·	·	·	·	·	·	5	·	·	·	·	·	·	·	·	·	·	·
LO CONGA	·	·	·	·	·	·	·	·	·	·	·	·	·	·	·	·	·	·	·	·	·	·	·	·	·	·	·	·	13	·	15	·

NOTES

TECHNO AFRICAN 32 STEPS

INSTRUMENT	1	2	3	4	5	6	7	8	9	10	11	12	13	14	15	16	1	2	3	4	5	6	7	8	9	10	11	12	13	14	15	16
O. HI-HAT	·	·	·	·	·	·	·	·	·	·	·	·	·	·	·	·	·	·	·	·	·	·	7	·	·	·	·	·	·	·	15	·
C. HI-HAT	·	·	·	·	·	·	·	·	·	·	·	·	·	·	·	·	·	·	·	·	·	6	·	8	·	·	·	·	·	14	·	16
SNARE DRUM	·	·	·	·	·	·	·	·	·	·	·	·	·	·	·	·	·	·	·	·	·	·	·	·	·	·	11	12	13	·	·	·
HI-TOM	·	·	·	·	·	·	·	·	·	·	11	12	13	·	·	·	·	·	·	·	·	·	·	·	·	·	·	·	·	·	·	·
BASS DRUM	1	·	·	·	·	·	7	8	9	·	·	·	·	·	15	·	·	·	·	·	·	·	7	8	9	·	·	·	·	·	·	·
CABASA	1	2	3	4	5	6	7	8	9	10	11	12	13	14	15	16	1	2	3	4	5	6	7	8	9	10	11	12	13	14	15	16
TIMBALES	·	·	·	·	5	·	·	·	·	·	·	·	13	·	·	·	·	·	3	4	·	·	·	·	·	·	11	12	·	·	15	16
HI CONGA	·	·	3	·	·	·	·	·	·	·	·	11	·	·	15	16	·	·	3	·	·	·	·	·	·	·	11	·	·	14	·	·
LO CONGA	·	·	·	·	·	·	7	8	·	·	·	·	·	·	15	16	·	·	·	·	·	·	·	·	·	·	·	·	·	·	15	16

NOTES

74

VOODOO 32 STEPS

INSTRUMENT	1	2	3	4	5	6	7	8	9	10	11	12	13	14	15	16	1	2	3	4	5	6	7	8	9	10	11	12	13	14	15	16
SNARE DRUM	·	·	·	·	5	·	·	·	·	·	·	·	13	·	15	·	·	·	·	·	5	·	·	·	·	·	·	·	13	14	15	·
BASS DRUM	1	2	3	·	·	·	·	8	·	10	11	·	·	·	·	·	1	2	3	·	·	·	·	8	·	10	11	·	·	·	·	·
CABASA	1	·	·	4	·	·	·	8	·	·	11	·	13	·	15	·	1	·	·	4	·	·	7	·	·	·	11	·	13	·	15	·
TIMBALES	·	·	·	·	5	·	·	·	·	·	·	·	13	·	15	·	·	·	·	·	5	·	·	·	·	·	·	·	13	14	15	·
HI CONGA	·	·	·	·	5	·	7	·	·	·	·	·	·	·	·	·	1	·	·	·	·	·	·	·	9	·	·	·	·	·	·	·
LOW CONGA	1	2	·	4	·	·	7	·	·	·	·	·	13	·	15	16	·	2	·	4	·	·	7	·	·	·	·	·	13	·	15	16

NOTES

SHUFFLE I 12 STEPS

INSTRUMENT	1	2	3	4	5	6	7	8	9	10	11	12
C. HI-HAT	1	·	3	·	·	·	7	·	9	·	·	·
O. HI-HAT	·	·	·	4	·	·	·	·	·	10	·	·
SNARE DRUM	·	·	·	·	·	·	7	·	·	·	·	·
BASS DRUM	1	·	·	·	·	6	·	·	·	·	·	12
ACCENT	·	·	·	·	·	·	·	·	·	·	·	·
CYMBAL	·	·	·	·	·	·	·	·	·	·	·	·
HANDCLAP	·	·	·	·	·	·	·	·	·	·	·	·

NOTES

SHUFFLE IV 12 STEPS

INSTRUMENT	1	2	3	4	5	6	7	8	9	10	11	12
C. HI-HAT	·	2	·	4	·	·	7	·	9	·	·	·
SNARE DRUM	·	·	·	·	·	·	·	·	·	10	11	·
TOM 1	1	·	·	·	·	·	·	·	·	·	·	·
TOM 2	·	·	3	·	5	6	·	·	·	·	·	12
TOM 3	·	·	·	·	·	·	·	8	·	·	·	·
BASS DRUM	1	·	·	4	·	·	7	·	·	10	·	·

NOTES

SHUFFLE II 12 STEPS

INSTRUMENT	1	2	3	4	5	6	7	8	9	10	11	12
C. HI-HAT	1	·	3	4	·	6	7	·	9	10	·	12
SNARE DRUM	·	·	·	4	·	·	·	·	·	10	·	·
BASS DRUM	1	·	·	4	·	·	7	·	·	10	·	·
ACCENT	1	·	·	4	·	·	7	·	·	10	·	·

NOTES

ROCK SHUFFLE 12 STEPS

INSTRUMENT	1	2	3	4	5	6	7	8	9	10	11	12
C. HI-HAT	1	2	3	4	5	6	7	8	9	10	11	12
SNARE DRUM	·	·	·	4	·	6	·	·	·	10	·	12
BASS DRUM	1	·	3	·	·	·	·	8	9	·	11	·
HANDCLAPS	·	·	·	4	·	6	·	·	·	·	·	12
ACCENT	1	·	·	4	·	6	·	·	·	10	·	·

NOTES

SHUFFLE III 24 STEPS

INSTRUMENT	1	2	3	4	5	6	7	8	9	10	11	12	1	2	3	4	5	6	7	8	9	10	11	12
COWBELL	1	·	·	·	·	·	7	·	·	·	·	·	1	·	·	·	·	·	7	·	·	·	·	·
C. HI-HAT	·	·	3	4	·	6	·	·	9	·	·	12	·	·	3	4	·	6	·	·	9	·	·	12
SNARE DRUM	·	·	·	·	·	·	·	·	·	10	·	·	·	·	·	·	·	·	·	·	·	·	·	·
TOM	·	·	·	·	·	·	·	·	·	·	·	·	·	·	·	·	·	·	·	·	·	10	·	·
BASS DRUM	1	·	·	·	·	6	·	·	·	·	·	·	1	·	·	·	·	6	·	·	·	·	·	·

NOTES

SHUFFLE V — 48 STEPS

BAR 1

INSTRUMENT	1	2	3	4	5	6	7	8	9	10	11	12	13	14	15	16	17	18	19	20	21	22	23	24
O. HI-HAT	·	·	·	4	·	·	·	·	·	10	·	·	·	·	·	16	·	·	·	·	·	22	·	·
C. HI-HAT	1	·	3	·	·	·	7	·	9	·	·	·	13	·	15	·	·	·	19	·	21	·	·	·
SNARE DRUM	·	·	·	·	·	·	7	·	·	·	·	·	·	·	·	·	·	·	19	·	·	·	·	·
BASS DRUM	1	·	3	·	·	·	·	·	·	·	·	·	13	·	15	·	·	·	·	·	·	·	·	·

BAR 2

INSTRUMENT	1	2	3	4	5	6	7	8	9	10	11	12	13	14	15	16	17	18	19	20	21	22	23	24
O. HI-HAT	·	·	·	4	·	·	·	·	·	10	·	·	·	·	·	16	·	·	·	·	·	22	·	·
C. HI-HAT	1	·	3	·	·	·	7	·	9	·	·	·	13	·	15	·	·	·	19	·	21	·	·	·
SNARE DRUM	·	·	·	·	·	·	7	·	·	·	·	·	·	·	·	·	·	·	19	·	·	·	·	·
BASS DRUM	1	·	3	·	·	6	·	·	9	10	·	·	13	·	15	·	·	·	·	·	·	·	·	·

NOTES

SHUFFLE FILL — 12 STEPS

INSTRUMENT	1	2	3	4	5	6	7	8	9	10	11	12
C. HI-HAT	·	2	·	4	·	·	7	·	9	·	·	·
SNARE DRUM	·	·	·	·	·	·	·	·	·	10	11	·
TOM 1	1	·	·	·	·	·	·	·	·	·	·	·
TOM 2	·	·	3	·	5	6	·	·	·	·	·	12
TOM 3	·	·	·	·	·	·	·	8	·	·	·	·
BASS DRUM	1	·	·	4	·	·	7	·	·	10	·	·

NOTES

SHUFFLE VI — 32 STEPS

INSTRUMENT	1	2	3	4	5	6	7	8	9	10	11	12	13	14	15	16	1	2	3	4	5	6	7	8	9	10	11	12	13	14	15	16
C. HI-HAT	1	·	·	4	5	·	·	8	9	·	·	12	13	·	·	16	1	·	·	4	5	·	·	8	9	·	·	12	13	·	·	16
SNARE DRUM	·	·	·	·	5	·	·	·	·	·	·	·	13	·	·	·	·	·	·	·	5	·	·	·	·	·	·	·	13	·	·	·
BASS DRUM	1	·	·	·	5	·	·	·	9	·	·	·	13	·	·	·	1	·	·	·	5	·	·	·	9	·	·	·	13	·	·	·

NOTES

BOSSANOVA I — 16 STEPS

INSTRUMENT	1	2	3	4	5	6	7	8	9	10	11	12	13	14	15	16
C. HI-HAT	1	2	3	4	5	6	7	8	9	10	11	12	13	14	15	16
O. HI-HAT	1	·	·	4	·	·	7	·	·	·	11	·	·	14	·	·
SNARE DRUM	·	·	·	·	·	·	·	·	·	·	·	·	·	·	·	·
BASS DRUM	1	·	·	4	5	·	·	8	9	·	·	12	13	·	·	16
ACCENT	·	·	·	·	5	·	·	·	·	·	·	·	13	·	·	·
CYMBAL	·	·	·	·	·	·	·	·	·	·	·	·	·	·	·	·
HANDCLAP	·	·	·	·	·	·	·	·	·	·	·	·	·	·	·	·

NOTES

BOSSANOVA II — 32 STEPS

INSTRUMENT	1	2	3	4	5	6	7	8	9	10	11	12	13	14	15	16	1	2	3	4	5	6	7	8	9	10	11	12	13	14	15	16
C. HI-HAT	1	·	3	·	5	·	7	·	9	·	11	·	13	·	15	·	1	·	3	·	5	·	7	·	9	·	11	·	13	·	15	·
SNARE DRUM	1	·	·	·	·	·	7	·	·	·	·	·	13	·	·	·	·	·	·	·	5	·	·	·	·	·	11	·	·	·	·	·
BASS DRUM	1	·	·	·	·	·	7	9	·	·	·	·	15	·			1	·	·	·	5	·	·	·	9	·	·	·	·	15	·	

NOTES

BOSSANOVA III — 16 STEPS

INSTRUMENT	1	2	3	4	5	6	7	8	9	10	11	12	13	14	15	16
C. HI-HAT	1	2	3	4	5	6	7	8	9	10	11	12	13	14	15	16
RIM SHOT	1	·	·	4	·	·	7	·	·	·	11	·	·	14	·	·
BASS DRUM	1	·	·	4	5	·	·	8	9	·	·	12	13	·	·	16

NOTES

SAMBA III — 16 STEPS

INSTRUMENT	1	2	3	4	5	6	7	8	9	10	11	12	13	14	15	16
C. HI-HAT	1	2	3	4	5	6	·	8	9	·	11	12	·	14	15	16
SNARE DRUM	1	·	3	·	5	6	·	8	·	10	11	·	13	14	·	16
BASS DRUM	1	·	·	4	5	·	·	8	9	·	·	12	13	·	·	16
ACCENT	·	·	·	·	·	·	·	8	·	·	·	12	·	·	·	·

NOTES

BOSSANOVA FILL — 16 STEPS

INSTRUMENT	1	2	3	4	5	6	7	8	9	10	11	12	13	14	15	16
RIDE	·	·	·	·	·	·	·	·	·	·	11	·	·	·	·	·
C. HI-HAT	1	2	3	4	5	6	7	8	·	10	·	·	·	·	·	·
SNARE DRUM	·	·	·	·	·	·	·	·	·	·	·	·	13	·	·	·
RIMSHOT	1	·	·	4	·	·	7	·	9	·	·	·	·	·	·	·
TOM 1	·	·	·	·	·	·	·	·	·	·	·	·	·	14	·	·
TOM 2	·	·	·	·	·	·	·	·	·	·	·	·	·	·	15	·
BASS DRUM	1	·	·	4	5	·	·	8	·	10	11	·	·	·	·	16

NOTES

SAMBA IV — 16 STEPS

INSTRUMENT	1	2	3	4	5	6	7	8	9	10	11	12	13	14	15	16
O. HI-HAT	·	·	·	·	·	·	·	8	·	·	·	·	·	·	·	·
C. HI-HAT	1	2	3	4	5	6	7	·	·	10	11	12	13	14	15	16
SNARE DRUM	1	·	3	·	5	·	·	8	·	10	·	12	·	·	15	·
TOM 3	·	·	·	·	5	·	·	·	·	·	·	·	13	·	·	·
BASS DRUM	1	·	·	4	·	·	·	8	9	·	·	12	13	·	·	16

NOTES

SAMBA I — 16 STEPS

INSTRUMENT	1	2	3	4	5	6	7	8	9	10	11	12	13	14	15	16
C. HI-HAT	1	2	3	4	5	6	7	8	9	10	11	12	13	14	15	16
O. HI-HAT	·	·	·	4	·	·	·	·	9	·	·	·	13	·	·	16
SNARE DRUM	1	·	·	4	5	·	·	·	·	10	·	12	13	·	·	·
BASS DRUM	1	·	·	4	5	·	·	8	9	·	·	12	13	·	·	16
ACCENT	1	·	·	4	5	·	·	8	9	·	·	12	13	·	·	16
CYMBAL	·	·	·	·	·	·	·	·	·	·	·	·	·	·	·	·
HANDCLAP	1	·	3	·	5	·	·	·	·	10	·	·	13	·	·	·

NOTES

SAMBA V — 16 STEPS

INSTRUMENT	1	2	3	4	5	6	7	8	9	10	11	12	13	14	15	16
O. HI-HAT	·	·	·	·	·	·	·	8	·	·	·	·	·	·	15	·
C. HI-HAT	1	2	3	4	5	6	7	·	·	10	11	12	13	14	·	·
SNARE DRUM	1	·	3	·	5	·	·	8	·	10	·	12	13	·	·	·
TOM 1	·	·	·	·	·	·	·	·	·	·	·	12	·	·	·	·
TOM 2	·	·	·	·	·	·	·	·	·	·	·	·	13	·	·	·
TOM 3	·	·	·	·	5	·	·	·	·	·	·	·	·	·	15	·
BASS DRUM	1	·	·	4	5	·	·	8	9	·	·	12	13	·	·	16

NOTES

SAMBA II — 16 STEPS

INSTRUMENT	1	2	3	4	5	6	7	8	9	10	11	12	13	14	15	16
O. HI-HAT	·	·	·	·	·	·	7	·	·	10	·	·	13	·	·	·
C. HI-HAT	1	2	3	4	5	6	·	8	9	·	11	12	·	14	15	16
BASS DRUM	1	·	·	4	5	·	·	8	9	·	·	12	13	·	·	16
ACCENT	1	·	·	·	5	·	·	·	9	·	·	·	·	·	·	·

NOTES

TANGO I — 16 STEPS

INSTRUMENT	1	2	3	4	5	6	7	8	9	10	11	12	13	14	15	16
C. HI-HAT	1	·	3	·	5	·	7	8	9	·	11	·	13	·	15	16
SNARE DRUM	·	·	·	·	·	·	·	8	·	·	·	·	·	·	·	16
BASS DRUM	1	·	3	·	5	·	7	8	9	·	11	·	13	·	15	16

NOTES

SAMBA FILL — 16 STEPS

INSTRUMENT	1	2	3	4	5	6	7	8	9	10	11	12	13	14	15	16
O. HI-HAT	·	·	·	·	·	·	·	·	·	·	·	·	·	·	·	16
C. HI-HAT	1	2	·	·	·	·	7	8	·	·	11	·	13	·	·	·
SNARE DRUM	·	·	3	·	5	·	·	·	9	·	·	12	·	·	15	·
TOM 1	·	·	3	·	5	·	·	·	·	·	·	·	·	·	·	·
TOM 2	·	·	·	·	·	·	·	·	9	·	·	·	·	·	·	·
TOM 3	·	·	·	·	·	·	·	·	·	·	·	12	·	·	15	·
BASS DRUM	1	·	·	4	5	·	·	8	9	·	·	12	13	·	·	16

NOTES

MAMBO I — 16 STEPS

INSTRUMENT	1	2	3	4	5	6	7	8	9	10	11	12	13	14	15	16
C. HI-HAT	1	·	·	4	5	·	7	·	9	·	11	·	13	·	·	·
O. HI-HAT	·	·	3	·	·	·	7	·	·	·	·	·	·	·	15	·
SNARE DRUM	·	·	·	·	·	·	·	·	·	·	·	·	·	·	·	·
BASS DRUM	1	·	·	·	·	·	7	·	·	·	·	·	13	·	·	·
ACCENT	·	·	·	·	·	·	·	·	·	·	·	·	·	·	·	·
CYMBAL	·	·	·	·	·	·	·	·	·	·	·	·	·	·	·	·
HANDCLAP	·	·	·	·	·	·	·	·	·	·	·	·	·	·	·	·

NOTES

TANGO II — 16 STEPS

INSTRUMENT	1	2	3	4	5	6	7	8	9	10	11	12	13	14	15	16
C. HI-HAT	1	·	·	·	5	·	·	·	9	·	·	·	13	·	·	·
O. HI-HAT	·	·	·	·	·	·	·	·	·	·	·	·	·	·	15	·
SNARE DRUM	1	·	·	·	5	·	·	·	9	·	·	·	13	·	15	·
BASS DRUM	1	·	·	·	5	·	·	·	9	·	·	·	13	·	15	·
ACCENT	1	·	·	·	5	·	·	·	9	·	·	·	13	·	15	·
CYMBAL	1	·	·	·	5	·	·	·	·	·	·	·	·	·	·	·
HANDCLAP	·	·	·	·	·	·	·	·	·	·	·	·	·	·	·	·

NOTES

MAMBO II — 16 STEPS

INSTRUMENT	1	2	3	4	5	6	7	8	9	10	11	12	13	14	15	16
C. HI-HAT	1	2	3	4	5	6	7	8	9	10	11	12	13	14	15	16
HI-CONGA	·	·	3	·	·	6	·	·	·	·	11	·	·	14	·	·
LO CONGA	·	·	·	·	·	·	7	8	·	·	·	12	·	·	15	16
BASS DRUM	1	·	·	4	5	·	7	·	9	·	·	12	13	·	15	·
CLAVES	1	·	3	·	5	·	7	·	9	·	11	12	13	·	15	16

NOTES

ROCK TANGO — 16 STEPS

INSTRUMENT	1	2	3	4	5	6	7	8	9	10	11	12	13	14	15	16
O. HI-HAT	·	·	·	·	·	·	·	·	·	·	·	·	·	·	15	·
C. HI-HAT	1	·	3	·	5	·	7	·	9	·	11	·	13	·	·	·
SNARE DRUM	1	·	·	·	5	·	·	·	·	·	·	·	·	·	15	·
TOM 1	·	·	·	·	·	·	·	·	9	·	11	·	·	·	·	·
TOM 2	·	·	·	·	·	·	·	·	·	·	·	·	13	14	15	·
BASS DRUM	1	·	·	·	5	·	·	·	9	·	·	12	·	·	15	·
ACCENT	1	·	·	·	5	·	·	·	9	·	·	12	13	·	15	·

NOTES

BEGUINE — 16 STEPS

INSTRUMENT	1	2	3	4	5	6	7	8	9	10	11	12	13	14	15	16
C. HI-HAT	1	2	3	4	5	6	7	8	9	10	11	12	13	14	15	16
HI-CONGA	·	2	·	4	·	6	·	8	·	10	·	12	·	14	·	16
LO-CONGA	1	·	·	·	5	·	7	·	9	·	·	·	13	·	15	·
BASS DRUM	1	·	·	·	5	·	7	·	9	·	·	·	13	·	15	·
CLAVES	1	·	·	4	·	·	7	·	·	·	11	·	13	·	·	·

NOTES

RHUMBA — 32 STEPS

INSTRUMENT	1	2	3	4	5	6	7	8	9	10	11	12	13	14	15	16	1	2	3	4	5	6	7	8	9	10	11	12	13	14	15	16
C. HI-HAT	1	·	3	4	5	·	7	·	9	·	11	·	13	·	15	·	1	·	3	4	5	·	7	·	9	·	11	·	13	·	15	·
HI-CONGA	1	·	·	·	·	·	7	·	9	·	·	·	·	·	·	·	1	·	·	·	·	·	7	·	9	·	·	·	·	·	15	·
LO-CONGA	·	·	·	·	·	·	·	·	·	·	·	·	13	·	15	·	·	·	·	·	·	·	·	·	·	·	·	·	13	·	15	·
BASS DRUM	1	·	·	·	·	·	·	·	9	·	·	·	13	·	·	·	1	·	·	·	·	·	·	·	9	·	·	·	13	·	·	·
CLAVES	1	·	·	·	·	·	7	·	·	·	·	·	13	·	·	·	·	·	·	·	5	·	·	·	9	·	·	·	·	·	·	·

NOTES

ENKA — 32 STEPS

INSTRUMENT	1	2	3	4	5	6	7	8	9	10	11	12	13	14	15	16	1	2	3	4	5	6	7	8	9	10	11	12	13	14	15	16
C. HI-HAT	1	·	3	4	5	·	7	·	9	·	11	·	13	·	15	·	1	·	3	4	5	·	7	·	9	·	11	·	13	·	15	·
BASS DRUM	1	·	·	·	·	·	7	·	9	·	·	·	13	·	·	·	1	·	·	·	·	·	7	·	9	·	·	·	13	·	·	·

NOTES

HABANERA — 16 STEPS

INSTRUMENT	1	2	3	4	5	6	7	8	9	10	11	12	13	14	15	16
C. HI-HAT	1	·	·	4	5	·	7	·	9	10	·	12	13	·	15	·
SNARE DRUM	·	·	·	·	·	·	7	·	·	·	·	·	·	·	15	·
BASS DRUM	1	·	·	4	5	·	7	·	9	10	·	12	13	·	15	·

NOTES

FOXTROT I — 16 STEPS

INSTRUMENT	1	2	3	4	5	6	7	8	9	10	11	12	13	14	15	16
C. HI-HAT	1	2	3	4	5	6	7	8	9	10	11	12	13	14	15	16
SNARE DRUM	·	2	·	4	·	6	·	8	·	10	·	12	·	14	·	16
BASS DRUM	1	·	3	·	5	·	7	·	9	·	11	·	13	·	15	·

NOTES

MARCH I — 16 STEPS

INSTRUMENT	1	2	3	4	5	6	7	8	9	10	11	12	13	14	15	16
C. HI-HAT	·	·	·	·	·	·	·	·	·	·	·	·	·	·	·	·
O. HI-HAT	·	·	·	·	·	·	·	·	·	·	·	·	·	·	·	·
SNARE DRUM	1	·	·	5	·	·	·	9	·	·	·	13	14	15	16	
BASS DRUM	1	·	·	·	·	·	·	9	·	·	·	·	·	·	·	
ACCENT	1	·	·	·	·	·	·	9	·	·	·	·	·	·	·	
CYMBAL	1	·	·	·	·	·	·	9	·	·	·	·	·	·	·	
HANDCLAP	·	·	·	·	·	·	·	·	·	·	·	·	·	·	·	·

NOTES

BALLAD I — 12 STEPS

INSTRUMENT	1	2	3	4	5	6	7	8	9	10	11	12
C. HI-HAT	1	2	3	4	5	6	7	8	9	10	11	12
RIM SHOT	·	·	·	4	·	·	·	·	·	10	·	·
BASS DRUM	1	·	·	·	·	6	7	·	·	·	·	12

NOTES

MARCH II — 32 STEPS

INSTRUMENT	1	2	3	4	5	6	7	8	9	10	11	12	13	14	15	16	1	2	3	4	5	6	7	8	9	10	11	12	13	14	15	16
SNARE DRUM	·	·	3	·	·	·	7	·	·	·	11	·	·	·	15	·	·	·	3	·	·	·	7	·	·	·	11	12	13	·	15	·
BASS DRUM	1	·	·	·	5	·	·	·	9	·	·	·	13	·	·	·	1	·	·	·	5	·	·	·	9	·	·	·	·	·	15	·

NOTES

BALLAD II — 24 STEPS

INSTRUMENT	1	2	3	4	5	6	7	8	9	10	11	12	1	2	3	4	5	6	7	8	9	10	11	12
C. HI-HAT	1	·	3	·	5	·	7	·	9	·	11	·	1	·	3	4	5	·	7	·	9	·	11	·
SNARE DRUM	·	·	·	·	·	·	7	·	·	·	·	·	·	·	·	·	·	·	7	·	·	·	·	·
BASS DRUM	1	·	·	·	·	·	·	·	·	·	11	·	1	·	·	·	·	·	·	·	·	·	11	·

NOTES

WALTZ I — 12 STEPS

INSTRUMENT	1	2	3	4	5	6	7	8	9	10	11	12
C. HI-HAT	1	·	3	·	5	·	7	·	9	·	11	·
O. HI-HAT	1	·	·	·	·	·	·	·	·	·	·	·
SNARE DRUM	·	·	·	·	5	·	·	·	9	·	·	·
BASS DRUM	1	·	·	·	·	·	7	·	·	·	11	·
ACCENT	1	·	·	·	5	·	·	·	·	·	11	·
CYMBAL	·	·	·	·	·	·	·	·	·	·	·	·
HANDCLAP	·	·	·	·	·	·	·	·	·	·	·	·

NOTES

JAZZ WALTZ I — 9 STEPS

INSTRUMENT	1	2	3	4	5	6	7	8	9
O. HI-HAT	·	·	3	·	·	·	7	·	·
C. HI-HAT	1	·	·	·	·	·	·	·	9
SNARE DRUM	·	·	·	·	·	·	·	·	9
TOM 2	1	·	·	4	·	·	·	·	·
TOM 3	·	·	·	·	·	6	·	·	·
BASS DRUM	1	·	·	·	·	6	7	·	·
ACCENT	·	·	3	·	·	·	·	·	·

NOTES

WALTZ-LIKE — 24 STEPS

INSTRUMENT	1	2	3	4	5	6	7	8	9	10	11	12	1	2	3	4	5	6	7	8	9	10	11	12
C. HI-HAT	·	·	·	·	·	·	·	·	·	·	·	·	·	·	3	·	5	·	7	·	·	·	·	·
RIM SHOT	·	·	·	·	·	·	7	·	·	·	·	·	·	·	·	·	5	·	·	·	·	·	·	·
BASS DRUM	1	·	·	·	·	·	·	·	·	·	·	·	1	·	·	·	·	·	·	·	·	·	·	·
CABASA	·	·	3	·	5	·	·	·	·	·	·	·	·	·	·	·	·	·	·	·	·	·	·	·
TAMBOURINE	·	·	·	·	·	·	·	·	9	·	·	·	·	·	·	·	·	·	·	·	9	·	·	·

NOTES

WALTZ II — 12 STEPS

INSTRUMENT	1	2	3	4	5	6	7	8	9	10	11	12
CYMBAL	1	·	3	·	5	·	7	·	9	·	11	·
SNARE DRUM	·	·	3	·	5	·	·	·	9	·	11	·
BASS DRUM	1	·	·	·	·	·	7	·	·	·	·	·

NOTES

ROCK WALTZ — 12 STEPS

INSTRUMENT	1	2	3	4	5	6	7	8	9	10	11	12
CYMBAL	1	·	·	·	·	·	·	·	·	·	·	·
C. HI-HAT	1	·	3	·	5	·	7	·	9	·	11	·
SNARE DRUM	·	·	3	·	5	·	·	·	9	·	11	·
BASS DRUM	1	·	·	·	·	·	7	·	·	·	·	12

NOTES

JAZZ WALTZ II — 24 STEPS

INSTRUMENT	1	2	3	4	5	6	7	8	9	10	11	12	1	2	3	4	5	6	7	8	9	10	11	12
CYMBAL	1	·	·	·	5	·	·	8	9	·	·	·	1	·	·	·	5	·	·	8	9	·	·	·
SNARE DRUM	·	·	·	·	5	·	·	·	9	·	·	·	·	·	3	·	·	·	·	·	9	·	·	·
BASS DRUM	1	·	·	·	·	·	·	·	·	·	·	·	1	·	·	·	·	·	·	·	9	·	·	·

NOTES